Boundary Layer

Library of Congress Cataloging-in-Publication Data

Names: Luther, Kem, 1946-
Title: Boundary layer / Kem Luther.
Description: Corvallis : Oregon State University Press, [2016] | Includes
    index.
Identifiers: LCCN 2015051035 (print) | LCCN 2016007274 (ebook) | ISBN
    9780870718441 (original trade pbk. : alk. paper) | ISBN 9780870718458
    (ebook)
Subjects: LCSH: Life zones. | Boundary layer (Meteorology)
Classification: LCC QH84 .L88 2016 (print) | LCC QH84 (ebook) | DDC
    578.09—dc23
LC record available at http://lccn.loc.gov/2015051035

Oregon State University Press
121 The Valley Library
Corvallis OR 97331-4501
541-737-3166 • fax 541-737-3170
www.osupress.oregonstate.edu

Boundary Layer

Exploring the Genius Between Worlds

∾

KEM LUTHER

Oregon State University Press   Corvallis

Also by Kem Luther
Cottonwood Roots

To Finn
who went outside with me
to see what we could see.

There is no such thing on earth as an uninteresting subject; the only thing that can exist is an uninterested person.

— G. K. Chesterton, *Heretics*

Contents

∾

Stegnon \'steg-nen\ n. pl. stegna. Biological chinking; a general term for all sessile microorganisms and meso-organisms (bacteria, fungi, algae, lichens, mosses, hepatics, etc.) that grow on or within the non-aquatic surfaces of the world, including rock, soil, and vegetation.
— Trevor Goward

∾

Preface

A European-derived culture thrust itself into the Pacific Northwest in the first half of the nineteenth century. Tens of thousands of settlers crowded onto the Oregon Trail and by the middle of the 1850s lands that North American aboriginals had managed for millennia suddenly had new managers.

The shift was delayed a bit on the Canadian side—Europeans were largely confined to Fort Langley on the mainland and Fort Victoria on Vancouver Island until the 1850s—but when it came, the change was as decisive as the one in the United States. If we had to pick a date for the management turnover in British Columbia, we might choose 1862, the year when smallpox killed half of the province's First Nations people.

The switch to new land managers in the Pacific Northwest is not an event, however, than can be pegged to a given year, either in the United States or in Canada. It happened over many decades. And it's still not over. As you read this, two dozen British Columbia lawyers are billing all of their hours to negotiating treaties to replace those that were signed during the turnover.

The proximity of these changes must come as a shock to the Old World historians who parcel out their narratives in centuries. As recently as a hundred years ago, hikers could head out on foot from Victoria or Seattle and find themselves, within a few hours, in nooks of nature that no European foot had touched, no European eye had seen. These near-in-time events, connected to us not only by what we read in books but also by stories handed down from parents and grandparents, condition how we think. The land retains an imprint of its aboriginal management and, beyond that, its self-management. The Pacific Northwest, it seems to me, is a kind of living laboratory. We run experiments here, sometimes without even knowing it, that probe how cultures coexist with nature. Our experiments are perhaps no different than those that are carried out in other regions of North America, but they seem more pressing here. The answers feel like they live nearer to the questions.

The experiments that we run in this living laboratory often employ the vocabulary and concepts of biology. Like most people who have a formal education, I reach for this vocabulary when I try to understand what we are learning. I'll make use of it on these pages, when I visit this living laboratory. I will also, however, test the limits of this language, and to do this I will have to stand in wider circles than the ones drawn by biologists.

My trips in this book, my hikes to the unexplored, will take us to strange places. We will not journey outward, into the lands on the horizon, but downward, into the *stegnon*, the land cover of mosses, lichens, fungi, and small plants. The significance of the Pacific Northwest's stegnon is, like the plankton in the ocean to the west of us, undervalued. It is also misunderstood. The words and concepts cultivated by the scientific community can, when applied to the stegnon, conceal as much as they reveal.

To light our way through this mysterious region, I employ the metaphor of a boundary layer. The first chapter of this book probes the metaphor itself. In the middle chapters, I chase this metaphor through local ecosystems. Pursuit of the metaphor brings us, in the end, to three boundary layers of a different type: the conceptual ones that lie between species and ecosystems, nature and culture, and science and the humanities.

Prandtl's Boundary Layer

I live in Metchosin, a rural community on the southern tip of Vancouver Island. My trips to the stegnon will begin here. Most of the trips will require a car, but this first one, a hike to explore the metaphor that will guide us on subsequent trips, takes me only a short distance from home.

It's early afternoon when I arrive at one of the little-used conservation areas near my house. I turn through a slow circle, scanning the horizon. No one in sight, no sound of anyone coming. I climb onto a car-sized boulder and stretch out, face down, on the damp green carpet that covers it.

These horizontal forays, I have found, are best done in places where I'm not likely to meet other people. The sight of a prone adult can be disturbing. When we chance on someone lying down in a public place in the middle of the day, our imaginations race through dire scenarios. Our first thought may be that the person is injured. We may also imagine some homeless person trying to nap or a drunk sleeping off the sins of the previous night. Thoughts of a corpse may edge into our minds. Even when the observer has eliminated the worst choices, the feeling persists that something not quite adult is going on. Children are the natural denizens of the layers just above the ground. When we release toddlers from our arms and deposit them on the ground, we train them to a direction. No one is surprised when they complete the downward motion. If an unhappy four-year-old sprawls on the floor of a mall, grownups walking by hardly break stride. At some point in our journey to adulthood, though, we lose the license to go low. I'm ready to explain, should anyone happen by, why I'm on the ground this morning. It's easier not to be asked.

A number of plants have colonized the rock I'm lying on. The first invaders would not, however, have been plants. They would have been crustose lichens, whose enzymes extract nutrient minerals and etch the hard surface. The lichens attract dust particles that build up small soil crusts in the rock crevices. The crusts give enough purchase for mosses to survive the assault of winds and rains. The decaying leaves and stems of the mosses transmute into more soil, enough to allow small vascular plants to survive.

The moss mat on this rock is made up largely of broom moss. Mixed in with the kelly green of broom moss is the darker green of juniper haircap, a moss whose individual stems resemble miniature pine trees. Sheltering in the boulder mosses are a few vascular plants: miner's lettuce, bedstraw, small mustards. I poke my finger into the green carpet and lever it back and forth until it hits rock. The thickest vegetative layer is about four centimeters. Not much, but perhaps the work of centuries.

Gusts of wind sway the Douglas-firs, alders, and red cedars above me. A light breeze swirls around me. Holding my hand at the level of my nose, I lower it toward the rock until my fingers no longer feel the movement of the wind. On this breezy morning the no-wind level is low, close to the tops of the mosses. The larger vascular plants around my rock, with their roots clamped in the soil and their tops lifting into the winds, connect the earth to the sky. Members of the stegnon—the carpet of green at the surfaces of soil, rock, and trees—dwell in a more restricted region. Their world is the centimeters-thin boundary layer.

The phrase *boundary layer* is a calque, a loanword that is translated literally when borrowed from another language. One of the better-known examples of a calque is the English phrase *blue blood*. We got the term by translating the Spanish phrase *sangre azul*. The Spanish peasants, who tended to have darker skin colors than other Europeans, called their upper-class rulers *sangres azules* because their blue veins stood out through their lighter skin. George Bernard Shaw gave us another popular calque when he imported the word *superman* from Nietzsche's *Übermensch*. And the French, from whom we borrowed the word *calque*, returned the favor by calling their skyscrapers *gratte-ciels*.

We calqued the phrase *boundary layer* from the writings of the German mathematician/engineer Ludwig Prandtl. Prandtl gave the world the earliest mathematical description of a *Grenzschicht* at a 1904 conference in Heidelberg, compounding the term from the German words for boundary and layer. Over the next three decades, his students made the phrase so popular that English-speaking scientists felt a need for an equivalent term in their own language.

Prandtl had practical motives for calling attention to *Grenzschichten*. In the same year that the mathematician delivered his paper on boundary layers, Orville Wright kept his *Flyer II* aloft for several minutes. In those days, the issue of powered flight was a topic of intense discussion wherever physicists and engineers gathered. The Wright brothers and other aeronautical inventors puzzled over wing designs for their new contraptions. When they posed the question of wing design to academics, engineers dusted off some centuries-old mathematical research. Isaac Newton had started to systematize the mathematics of fluids and friction, without much success, in the second book of his 1687 *Principia Mathematica*. Leonhard Euler put hydrodynamics on firmer mathematical footing in the next century, but his equations ignored viscosity, the way the density of air and other liquids affects the objects they flow over. By the nineteenth century the French engineer Claude-Louis Navier and the English evangelical George Stokes had adjusted the equations of Newton and Euler to account for viscosity. The result, however, was an imposing series of nonlinear differential equations that could not be solved with the calculating tools available in the early 1900s. The Wright brothers, lacking any realistic way to analyze the results of their wing designs on paper, were forced to carry out trial-and-error experiments in a home-made wind tunnel. The situation, however, was about to change. By the 1920s, mathematical tools to calculate the performance of the various wing and body designs became available to aeronautical researchers. The tools would continue to be refined during the colonization of the air that became an overriding passion of the twentieth century. Behind every set of formulas was Prandtl's pioneering work on boundary layers.

Though the mathematical vocabulary of Prandtl's 1904 paper is dense, the observations behind the analysis are sturdy and simple. When a fluid such as air flows over the surface of a hard object, such as a sphere, it finds itself sandwiched between two sets of Newtonian principles, one governing the object, the other the fluid. Between these two systems of mathematical regularity lies a small region where the laws of the two systems mix. It was the genius of Prandtl to observe that this region, the boundary layer, was relatively small. At the windward edge of a ten-centimeter ball, the boundary layer is only one or two millimeters thick. He also pointed out that the boundary layer has its own rules, patterns that can be isolated from the systems around it. Within the narrow boundary layer, for example, wind speeds, which vary from zero at the surface of the sphere up to the speed of the passing air at the top edge of the layer, ratchet upward in predictable steps. The changes are regular, but not linear: as the distance from the surface of the sphere increases, the rate of change in the wind speed slows down.

The thinness of the boundary layer, coupled with the fact that speed transitions within the boundary layer follow preset patterns, means that we can isolate certain flow problems, setting them apart from the general case. The result is that the number of variables in our descriptions of these special cases is reduced. This sort of number packaging makes mathematicians happy. It also pleases aeronautical engineers, because happy mathematicians show them how to write computer programs to analyze airfoil performance, programs that cost only a fraction of what they would have had to pay for a wind tunnel.

By the time World War II started, Prandtl's insights had become an integral part of the science of hydrodynamics and scientists in other fields were beginning to notice something similar to the boundary layers of the aeronautical engineers in their own disciplines. Meteorologists defined what they called the *planetary boundary layer*, the part of the atmosphere that is directly affected by the surface of the earth. Oceanographers began to talk about the *oceanic boundary layer*, the horizontal slice of water that responds most rapidly to changes in the air at the upper bound of the ocean.

This morning, the start of a blustery February day, I'm smack in the middle of a meteorological boundary layer. The weather forecast called for wind speeds of thirty kilometers per hour and gusts to fifty. But these predictions describe the steady winds that flow far above my head, not the discombobulated winds near the ground. How high we have to go in order to experience what the forecasts predict can vary—the top of the planetary boundary layer moves up and down, depending on time of day, air temperature, and surface irregularities. In the hundred meters of air closest to the ground, wind speeds don't usually match what the meteorologists describe. I roll onto my back and watch the winter winds pirouette along the upper boughs of the trees. The weather up there is not the weather I'm experiencing down here.

Boundary layers, it seems to me, are more common than aeronautical engineers, oceanographers, and meteorologists imagine. To make a boundary layer, all we need is a pair of large, stable systems of regularity that rub against each other. Where they come into contact, the two systems create a third region that is unstable, at least from the viewpoint of someone residing inside one of the larger systems. But boundary layers—and this is the key to all boundary layers—do not give in to the raw instability that gives rise to them. They fight back, making and enforcing their own laws. By giving attention to these unique regions and the regularities that appear in them, we can, like Prandtl, simplify our ways of thinking about the conflicts between large, stable systems. Where we once saw only chaos, we begin to see order.

In the coming months, I will follow this metaphor of a boundary layer to see where it leads, to learn what chaos it can conquer. My first appointment is on the northwest corner of Vancouver Island, near the tourist resorts of Tofino.

Hishuk ish ts'awalk.
Everything is one, interconnected.
— Nuu-chah-nulth saying

❧

Disappearing Dunes

A cold rain slants in from the ocean. Wind-driven drops pock the sands of Long Beach. Three of us trudge single file, heads down, toward the Wickaninnish Beach dunes. Danielle Bellefleur, a Parks Canada biologist, and Carl Sieber, an interpreter for Pacific Rim National Park Reserve, are dressed for the biting winds. I'm not so well prepared. Today, Carl says, is "seasonal," a weasel word for a March day at the eastern edge of the northern Pacific. I shiver and hitch tighter my thin raincoat.

Danielle Bellefleur (left) and Carl Sieber at Wickaninnish Beach dunes.

Weather is only one of the challenges on these open beaches. To-night an earthquake off the coast of Japan will heave up a Pacific-wide tsunami. In Japan, the displaced water will slaughter people by the tens of thousands. Here, no one will die—the fast-moving swell will be barely a meter high after it crosses the ocean, an almost unnoticeable blip among the two-meter waves pounding the beach. Only when I return home to the southern tip of the island and see the video feeds coming in from Japan will I grasp the magnitude of the event.

I've come to Long Beach in Canada's Pacific Rim National Park Reserve to visit a boundary layer. A highly specialized ecosystem, sand-wiched between vast reaches of land and ocean, has taken hold in the dunes above the beach. Danielle is running a five-year project to save this ecosystem from human-induced threats. Her friend Carl conveys the nuances of this struggle to people who have thought about the beach only in terms of sun, sand, scenes, and surf.

Earlier today I sat down with Danielle to learn more about dune eco-systems and to prepare for what we would see this afternoon. Somewhere in the detail of our discussion, I lost the bigger picture, but now, with an angry ocean to my left and sleeping dunes to my right, I remember why I'm here. Boundary layers are regions of high dynamism. Straddled between two contiguous regions, with each region trying to enforce its laws, these marginal areas write their own rules.

While my companions pause to examine several strange cavities next to a beach log, I step back to survey the beach. A battle is being fought here, and the weapons of choice are small rocks. A single grain of sand is not much of a threat—the stony missiles are only about a tenth of a millimeter across—but when wave action lifts them in large numbers and nudges them landward, the tiny rocks can sculpt the face of the land. Building beaches out of these grains takes time, of course. The gentler waves waft sand inward and the stronger storm waves yank the sand back. Here at Long Beach the smaller waves are winning this millennial tug of war. In certain sections of Pacific Rim National Park Reserve, the beach grows by tens of centimeters each year.

Water moves sand onto this beach. When the sand dries out, the onshore breezes take over and keep the sand in motion. The wind speed at ground level, we know, is always zero. How, then, does wind grab sand from a flat beach? The answer lies in the scale. On a level beach in a strong wind, the line that defines negligible wind speed—the top of the boundary layer—is only about a thirtieth of the height of an average grain of sand. When wind speeds reach about sixteen kilometers per hour, the force of the wind begins to move the sand. At first the little stones barge and roll along the surface. As the wind speed increases, some grains begin what physicists call *saltation*. The sand rises into the air, picks up speed, and crashes onto the beach. The acquired energy of the flying grains displaces other grains of sand, which saltate in turn. A strong wind gives rise to a Lilliputian sandstorm, a saltation cloud, that can move great volumes of sand over and off the beach. There's not much sand movement today. Rain has dampened the grains, gluing them in place. When the sun comes out, though, the beach sand will resume its march away from the ocean.

Wind-driven sand gives rise to the ecosystem that I have come to Wickaninnish to see. The ocean-side border of this system is marked by the high tide line. The beach below the tide line, where we are walking now, is a botanical desert. Single-celled algae can make a go of it on wave-lapped beaches, and the occasional vascular plant will hold out long enough to set seed, but terrestrial plants only begin to shape themselves into a full ecosystem in places where waves do not pay regular visits.

When we reach the entrance to the Wickaninnish dunes, Carl and Danielle veer away from the ocean and lead me across the tide line and up a sand ridge. At the top of the ridge we find ourselves, quite suddenly, in a different world. A sparse garden of wintering plants reaches away to the east, ending, some hundred meters ahead, at a line of trees atop a rising mound of sand. We are standing, says Danielle, on the foredune, the ridge nearest the ocean. This is where leapfrogging grains of sand make their first stop.

Foredunes are the work of pioneering plants, mostly varieties of grass. The tops of the plants force the line of negligible wind speed to angle up from the ground, making it harder for beach winds to loft the uppermost grains. The tough roots of the grasses also play a role, seizing the sand, binding it in place. The moving sand grains, checking in at the line of grass but not checking out, build themselves into a foredune mound. When storm waves at high tide batter this mound, the angle of the seaward slope can increase, sometimes becoming an almost vertical wall. Most of the sand beaches in the Pacific Northwest have these foredunes. On the Pacific beaches in the United States, some foredunes rise ten meters above the tops of the beaches. The ones here on Long Beach can reach four or five meters.

On the leeward side of the foredune ridge, the sand blowing in from the beach and cresting the foredune gives rise to a dune system, a theater in which moving sand is the producer, director, and lead actor. Dune systems can reach several kilometers into the land, but most are measured, as the ones at Long Beach are, by the tens of meters. Some dune systems along the Pacific Coast are marked by relatively flat sand plains, others have a series of modest dune ridges separated by plains and swales. The sand makes its last, wind-driven leap at the system's eastward edge, where high retention ridges can rise. At the tops of the ridges, where the force of wind and sand are no longer a factor, forest ecosystems begin to assert themselves.

Unique communities of plants have adapted themselves to the harsh environment between the beach and the forest. The local flora in these communities responds, as plants do everywhere, to changes in temperature, light, fertility, acidity, and moisture. Plants here also have to deal with two other challenges that the majority of plants can ignore: salt and sand.

The plants encounter salt that is left behind on the sand when seawater evaporates. But salt can also stage an air attack. Wave action creates bubbles that rise to the ocean surface and pop, flinging aloft salt-laden drops. The wind blasts this salt spray against nearby vegetation. Many of the dune plants have evolved, as we might imagine, a high tolerance for salt.

Roving sand can also make life difficult for dune system plants. Most vascular plants assume the existence of a stable soil level. Below the soil level they develop organs for collecting and storing water and nutrients. Above the soil they have organs for gathering sunlight and cooking up essential carbon compounds. On the dunes, these assumptions no longer hold: on one day the sand might expose the tender roots of plants growing in it, the next day it might heap itself against the aboveground organs, in extreme cases even burying the whole plant. Plants that colonize dune systems have, by necessity, special adaptations that let them cope with the vagaries of moving sand. Some are so well adapted that, when sand stops trying to cover them, they exhibit a form of plant puzzlement, slowing and even retracting their growth.

Carl and Danielle begin to point out the denizens of these dunes. We find the partly exposed, fleshy roots of yellow sand-verbena. A black knotweed is ready to unfurl its needlelike leaves. Scattered tufts of beach bluegrass have retained their green hue through the winter. Here and there, corpses of large-headed sedge show us where the plants' perennial roots will press up new flowers in a month or so. This is still late winter, though, and many of the more spectacular dune plants are not out yet. Today we see no sign of the beach-carrots, beach morning-glories, and gray beach peavines that Carl will highlight on his walks with the late spring and summer crowds. The visitors do not see, never will see, the mats of soil fungi that underpin this thriving plant community. Mycologists probing these sands typically find a half dozen or more species of fungi associated with each plant. Without the help of these fungi to solicit water and nutrients from the grudging sand, few of these dune system plants could survive.

Three Wickaninnish dunes beach plants in early summer (left to right): yellow sand-verbena, beach-carrot, beach morning glory.

The species count of plants in these dune communities is relatively low. A tally of species in the nearby forest would easily exceed the number that live here. What the dune species lack in quantity, however, they make up in quality. Many of the species that call these swales of sand their home are endemic to dune ecosystems—they occur nowhere else—and several of these dune endemics are rare and endangered. The gray beach peavine is a good example. Two islands, Vancouver Island and Haida Gwaii, have about ten thousand gray beach peavine plants. The rest of Canada can claim only two hundred more.

The poster child for these rare dune plants is pink sand-verbena. In the first decades of the twentieth century, botanists reported several populations of the plant along the western beaches of Vancouver Island. Then pink sand-verbena disappeared, apparently overwhelmed by invasive competitors and by development pressures on the beach ecosystems where it lived. Botanical manuals published twenty years ago report it as vanished. About ten years ago, however, a woodsman living along an isolated stretch of the West Coast Trail came across a single pink sand-verbena. He found it on a dune near the old native settlement of Cheewaht, a place accessible only by boat or by a grueling two-day hike along the West Coast Trail. Over the next few years, the plant continued to return to the same spot and he was able to collect some of its seeds. Then it disappeared. A few years ago greenhouse plants raised from the collected seeds were used to restart the Cheewaht population. In 2010, pink sand-verbena suddenly popped up on its own in two locations that were sixty kilometers north of Cheewaht, near Long Beach. Danielle and other biologists speculate that the long-lived, seawater-hardy seeds of pink sand-verbena account for both the return of the plant to Cheewaht ten years ago and the recent migration of the plant from Cheewaht to the new sites. During its eons of evolution on the unforgiving dunes, this plant species has acquired an unusual skill: it has learned the trick of living, for decades at a time, without the support of its ecosystem.

The return of pink sand-verbena is a happy-ending story within a larger tale of woe. The rarer dune plants have had, overall, a bad century. Besides the usual challenges from the broad natural stabilities that border their narrow realm, four human activities have proved troublesome. At one time agriculture and mining nipped at these fragile areas. The politically strategic location of beaches and their contiguous dunes have also brought them to military attention. Wickaninnish, for example, was the site of army exercises during and after World War II. Carl stoops to retrieve a piece of metal from the sand. The base plug of a grenade, he explains, showing us with his balled fist how the fragment slotted into the weapon. The most pressing threat to dune systems, though, is no longer the trio of agriculture, mining, and military: it is the relentless expansion of residential communities. In the United States, 70 percent of people going on vacation head for a beach. A million tourists make their way to the west side of Vancouver Island each year, most coming to swim at the beaches and stroll the sands. The annual stampede of summer visitors to beach areas gives rise to year-round support services that encroach on the dunes. Hotels, residences, recreational facilities, gas stations, restaurants, access roads—all need their tract of land near the beach. In popular tourist areas, the only dune plant communities still intact are ones that are either inaccessible to humans or ones that shelter in parks and nature reserves. Not even restricted access guarantees preservation: scientists in the Netherlands have found that intensive fossil fuel use in neighboring countries adds an extra thirty kilograms of nitrogen to each hectare of their protected dune systems. The nitrogen sifting out of the air interferes with the finely balanced nutritional adaptations of dune plants.

What brings us to Wickaninnish today is another face of the threat posed by human proximity to dune ecosystems. Danielle shows me two foredunes, one about two meters above the tide line, the other dominated by scattered, meter-high humps. The tall one has been built up by a pair of plants that humans brought here, European and American beachgrasses, *Ammophila arenaria* and *Ammophila breviligulata*. The other foredune, the collection of small mounds, is populated by a native grass, dune wildrye (*Leymus mollis*).

The nonnative beachgrasses were planted on Pacific beaches to solve a problem. The migrating dunes along the oceans interfered with human occupation. Sand from the dunes blocked the settlers' roads, clogged their machinery, buried their crops, and banked against their houses. The native grasses did not form foredunes large enough to halt sand movement. European beachgrass, immigrants knew, could stop the sand.

Residents of California began planting European beachgrass as early as the 1860s. Between 1930 and 1960, the US government underwrote the planting of thousands of hectares of the stabilizing invader. Beachgrass quickly adapted to the new environment and started to spread on its own. Today, most of the dune ecosystems on the northwest coast of North America are colonized by European beachgrass.

In places where the beachgrass-trapped sand stops moving inland, native dune plants begin to disappear and competitor species, once held at bay by the moving sand, start to encroach. Hard on the heels of the new colonizers come forests, trudging in some cases right up to the beach. Carl directs my attention to the foredune wall of beachgrass that we walked along on our way to the Wickaninnish dune systems. Low shrubs of kinnikinnick and salal mat the sands behind the foredune wall. Small trees have taken hold. The high foredune, blocking the airborne sands, no longer permits the dune areas behind the wall to host healthy communities of native dune plants.

The disappearing dunes. Sands behind the foredune wall of Ammophila *have been completely populated by trees and low shrubs.*

The planting of European beachgrasses on the northern Pacific coasts began to slow in the 1960s when the expansion of ecosystem knowledge—a topic we will take up in a later chapter—brought fresh attention to the threatened dune systems. Botanical surveys of the dunes demonstrated that more beachgrass meant fewer native species. Several of the native plants, researchers soon discovered, were perilously close to extinction. Programs to plant beachgrass were halted. By the 1990s, ecologists were pondering a further step. Could some of the beachgrass-inflicted damage, they wondered, be reversed?

∾

Earlier today I brought my questions about the *Ammophila* war to the warden's office at Pacific Rim Park Reserve. No one is at the reception desk when I arrive. I thump the knob of a bellhop bell. A white-haired man appears and leads me through a rabbit warren of offices and into a long conference room. Tacked up around the walls are 2005 Landsat photographs of Vancouver Island's western coasts. After a few minutes Danielle Bellefleur, clutching a sheaf of aerial photographs, joins me in the conference room.

We slide two chairs into a corner. "I'll see the results of the beach-grass program on the dunes this afternoon," I say. "Tell me about what we won't see—the history, the science."

Danielle shuffles the papers she brought as she thinks about how to put the topic in perspective. "*Ammophila*, beachgrass, is not the only problem faced by these ecosystems. Beach logs also change the dunes. The logs on our beaches are detritus from the peak in logging thirty or more years ago. Logging in this area is declining, though, so we expect logs to be less of a problem in the future. Direct human activity also threatens the dunes. Walking on the sand is not usually a problem—the plants have deep roots and can recover. But campfires from illegal overnight campers can hurt plant communities. On some of our busiest summer days, I can see remnants of a dozen campfires from the night before. The fires can wipe out the native plant seeds that are banked in the sand. At least, though, Pacific Rim doesn't have the ATV problems that some of the Oregon dunes have. Powered machines can cause immense destruction.

"Ecologists have known for some time that *Ammophila* also threatens the survival of the native sand ecosystems. The plant communities we have on Long Beach are adapted to a moving sand environment. The local foredune grasses, such as *Leymus mollis* and the poas, encourage this environment. They build up small domes that the sand can pass over and between. *Ammophila*, in contrast, builds up walls that stop the sand, choking off the dune systems above the beach. *Leymus* plays well with others. *Ammophila* doesn't.

"Attempts to remove *Ammophila* got started in the United States. Biologists there tried several removal techniques. Herbicides, they found, didn't work well. In one experiment, seawater was pumped directly onto the *Ammophila*. The salt water had some effect, but the process was too costly to scale up. Manual removal of beachgrass proved too difficult. Park managers finally decided on mechanical removal—they used an excavator to dig up and bury the *Ammophila*. The largest mechanical removal project has been carried out at California's Lanphere Dunes in what is now Humboldt Bay National Wildlife Refuge. It started in the 1990s. Results from that study convinced the restoration community that *Ammophila* removal could work."

"This program to do a test removal of beachgrass on Vancouver Island—how did it get started? How did you get involved?" I ask.

"I backed into the project. My background was in biology. I did a master's degree in biology at Dalhousie, working with communities in the Philippines on a local marine protected area for my thesis. I started at Parks Canada as a biologist. I wanted to get outside more, though, so I switched over to warden duties. I was stationed briefly at Kejimkujik Park in Nova Scotia, then at Jasper Park in the Canadian Rockies. After I arrived here in 2001, I began to shift back toward the biology and ecology side of park activities, doing biology projects in the winter, warden work in the summers. The biology side gradually took over. Now I'm what Parks Canada calls an environmental assessment officer.

"When I began doing biology at Pacific Rim Park, I didn't know much about dune ecosystems. The person that encouraged the staff here to think about what was happening on the dunes was a Parks Canada

employee named Barry Campbell. He assembled a group of young workers to do *Ammophila* pulls. They managed to open up a small channel
for beach sand in one of the Wickaninnish foredunes. One summer my
husband and I came to the beach—a picnic to celebrate our first wed-
ding anniversary—and Barry showed up. He told us about the *Ammophila*
project. Then he took us to the dunes behind the beach to show us
how yellow sand-verbena was already returning in the areas where the
sand had started to move. That got me started researching dune ecology issues. I teamed up with Phil Lee, a Parks Canada ecologist who
did his PhD work on the dunes, and we received some initial money to
do a baseline study of the plant communities in the dunes. Then Parks
launched a five-year test restoration project using mechanical *Ammophila*
removal. We're in the third year of the program. About three-quarters of
the *Ammophila* has been removed from the target area."

"Mechanical removal? How do you use machines to get rid of the
beachgrass?"

"We have an excavator with a special comb attachment. It digs down
below the *Ammophila* and pulls the whole plant, roots and all, out of the
sand. Then we open up a pit and bury the plants and roots so deep
that the *Ammophila* can't regenerate. The year after the initial mechanical
removal, *Ammophila* tries to come back from banked seeds and from the
root fragments we missed, but the stands are so weak that hand removal
is practical. Each year after, less and less *Ammophila* tries to return."

"And after you remove the high foredunes, you replant native
species?"

"We do very little replanting. Once it has space to grow, the native
community rapidly restores itself. Our posttreatment sampling is supposed to start next year, but we can already see native plants coming into
the area where we have removed the *Ammophila* and into the dunes where
the sand has started to move."

"When did the *Ammophila* become a problem at Long Beach?"

"*Ammophila* began to take hold, we believe, in the 1960s. A botanist
studying vegetation here in 1972 noted the presence of *Ammophila*, but
reported it as patchy." Danielle thumbs two photographs from her sheaf
of pictures and points out the Wickaninnish section on each one. "One
photograph is a recent aerial shot. The other was taken in the 1960s.

In the recent photo you can see how extensive *Ammophila* foredunes have built up. You can also see how the cover of trees and shrubs in the backdune area has increased. We think the high foredunes have been responsible for the loss of the open backdunes.

"We're focusing our removal efforts on Wickaninnish Beach. But the initial invasion of *Ammophila* may have happened farther north." Danielle runs her finger along the beach line on the more recent photograph. "This part of Long Beach is Combers Beach. We call it 'the uterus for invasive species.' Sandhill Creek exits at Combers. In summers the creek would turn and run parallel to the beach for a hundred meters. In winters the higher waters in the river would punch through onto the beach directly across from the main stream. Over the years, *Ammophila* built up the foredune berm so high that the creek waters could no longer break through. The backed-up waters started to invade a parking lot that we had constructed on the site of an old lodge. Eventually the redirected creek forced us to remove the parking lot. We had to construct an expensive new lot and reroute a beach trail."

"Has documenting this sort of damage made it easier to find funding for *Ammophila* removal projects?" I ask.

"I would say that we are behind the US. We still haven't made the Canadian public aware of the dangers posed by *Ammophila*. In some places, owners of beach properties may still be planting beachgrass to stabilize beaches. When the word began to get around about our project, a manager of one of the local hotels called me and asked if he could have the beachgrass that we were removing!

"The long-term success of this project depends on the public coming to understand and value what we are doing. This is why we have included a large public education segment in our project. In the summers, Carl leads walks onto the dunes and explains what is happening. Education on these interpretive walks flows in two directions. Those who are concerned about the preservation of ecological systems can be alarmed when they see heavy machinery on the beach. They need to know what we are doing and why we are doing it. Those who haven't thought much about human impact on the dune environments need to understand what we have lost."

"What will happen if the beachgrass is not removed?"

Danielle points again at the Wickaninnish area in the latest photo. "One of our researchers used the differences between the earlier and later photos to project the changes into the future. All of the dune complexes where we are removing *Ammophila*, he computed, will be completely closed off by 2030 if we do nothing. It's tough to think about having a dead dune only fifteen or twenty years from now."

∿

After we have walked around the dunes, Danielle and Carl lead me back toward the beach to show me the strip where excavators did their work last fall. Wind and waves have erased any evidence of the gouges made by the machines. Winter blasts have already carried huge amounts of sand through the opened channel. The dunes behind have begun to walk, reclaiming an ancient boundary region between land and water.

Danielle has a meeting in about an hour, so we start back to the parking lot. Instead of hiking back along the beach, we turn away from the ocean and walk through the dunes until we intersect a forest path. On the way, I ask Carl how visitors react to his dune walks. Carl's experience with park interpretation, it turns out, is both wide and deep. His father was a park superintendent and Carl grew up in a series of Canadian national parks, starting with Auyuittuq, the "land that never melts," on Baffin Island and ending up at Mount Revelstoke in the Canadian Rockies. After experimenting with other careers, including teaching and acting, he gave in to his genetic programming and returned to Parks Canada as an interpreter.

"The dune walk is not an easy sell to visitors. We've had to put a lot of thought, not only into the program itself, but into how to attract people to the program. One method we use is to link the dune walk to more popular outings. We might, for example, have an interpreter take people on a seashore wander. Fifteen minutes into the walk I meet the group and the interpreter says 'Here's Carl, who will take you to the dunes behind the beach.'

"Once we get people to the dunes, we have to provide more story than our other trips require. On a walk through a forest, the forest contributes to the narrative. An old-growth spruce is its own 'wow' moment.

It has been there for a long time and conveys a sense of permanence. The dunes are more transient, less imposing. We have to shape a narrative that links the dune story and the lives of the visitors. On a windy day, we point out, you can stand for a few minutes and watch small dunes form around your feet. When we alter the dunes—as we are doing with the *Ammophila* project—the results come quickly. Visitors who return to the park a few years after a forest walk won't see many changes to the forest, but those who return to the dunes will see lots of changes, both the ones that we are making and the ones that the ecosystem itself triggers. The narrative thread on the dune walks becomes a story of natural change and how humans interact with it."

Danielle stops in the forest and points at a small hill. "That's an old foredune. It tells us that at some point the water level was higher or the land was lower."

I think about the westward expansion of the beach. "Couldn't it be the remnants of a retention ridge?"

"We think it's a foredune," says Carl. "We can tell that water came this far up. On this coast there are clams—piddocks—that drill into rock to make their home. They live below the tide line. Along the rocky parts of our shoreline, high above the tide line, you can find holes in rock where these clams once lived. The line between ocean and land moves."

∽

A month after my day at the Wickaninnish dunes, while I'm reading about the dune ecosystems of the northern Pacific coasts, the old foredune in the forest comes to mind. If Carl and Danielle are right, at some time in the last few millennia land and water met at a beach that was a dozen meters higher than the current beach—a strong reminder, if we needed it, that tasks of conservation and restoration often occur in unstable environments.

No one has understood the instability of dune ecosystems better than Alfred M. Wiedemann, an iconoclastic scientist who spent over forty years studying the geology, botany, and zoology of the northern Pacific beaches. He was a faculty member at Evergreen State College in Olympia, Washington. When Wiedemann examined the *Ammophila* issue in the 1990s, he posed the beachgrass problem against a deep historical background. The control of *Ammophila*, he concluded, "may be feasible over small areas for specific purposes, such as habitat restoration," but management of plant populations would have little effect on the "natural cyclic processes" that periodically convulse the dunes.

Employing data from C^{14}, thermoluminescence tests, and drilling cores, Wiedemann determined that there were two base layers to the northern Pacific dunes. One was laid down at the end of the last ice age, the other four thousand years ago, about the time the sea reached its current level. In subsequent centuries, he found, the dune regions were stabilized several times, in some cases to the point of supporting mature forests and larger trees, before being overrun by sand. When Wiedemann combined several independent geological studies of the Oregon dunes and mapped them onto a timeline, he discovered that periods of stability have been regularly interrupted over large swaths of northern Pacific beaches and dunes. The interruptions occurred every four to six centuries.

What caused these destabilizing events? The article is not very specific. I want to know more. Wiedemann died last year, but he wrote the *Ammophila* article with a younger colleague, Andrea Pickart. She is an ecologist at California's Humboldt Bay National Wildlife Refuge. I call her up and ask whether more work has been done on Wiedemann's "natural cyclic processes" since they wrote the article. "Oh, yes," she

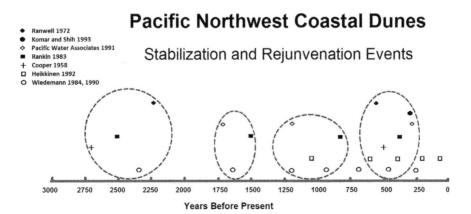

Timing of dune destabilization events. This image, which is similar to one that Pickart and Wiedermann published in the 1990s, is courtesy of Andrea Pickart.

says, "there has been a lot more work on this topic by the geologic community. Major earthquakes on the Cascadia subduction zone—we are on the very southern end of it here in California—are the culprit. They happen every three to six hundred years and lead to large tsunamis, just as they did in Japan last month. Our last big earthquake was in 1700. We can date it almost to the hour because the tsunami that it caused was still powerful when it hit Japan. People there recorded the time of the event."

As the Pacific Ocean plates dive under the continent along the western coastlines of the Americas, they scrape against the underside of the continental plates. Friction between the two layers is high and the land masses lock together. The continental plate, like a blanket on a bedsheet being moved under it, crinkles and pooches where it overrides the diving oceanic plate. The land near the ocean, as a result, slowly rises. When the plate tensions get too high, friction can no longer hold the plates together and they suddenly unlock and slide against each other. In the resulting spasm the continent slips westward and sighs lower just as a wall of water generated by undersea sections of the slippage drives onto the land. Pulses of tsunami waves scour away sand, soil, and rocks. Because the land is now lower and onshore barriers have been removed, the ocean margin creeps toward the continent. After the recent earthquake and tsunami in Japan, the slumped land turned high tide into a daily menace along sections of the seashore. The problem will right itself in coming decades, as the aftershocks subside and the plates relock. The locking will force the land plate to rise and the tide line will resume its march toward the ocean.

This periodic rising and falling of the shore can make it difficult to read the larger story written on the land. The old foredune, now hundreds of meters from water, summarizes it for us. The dune may have formed at the start of one of the stabilizing periods. Over several centuries local crustal rebound lifted the land and further additions of sand moved the shoreline to the west. At the height of the stabilization, a forest overgrew the foredune. Held in place by bulky plant material and lifted above and to the east of the area of regular destruction, that section of old foredune survived the next cycle (or cycles) of destabilizing events.

I have heard that the effects of the recent Japanese earthquake had been more noticeable in California than they were farther north. I ask

Andrea if the area around the Lanphere Dunes had been touched by the tsunami. "It certainly affected public opinion," she says. "Right now we are experiencing a period of community backlash—from some of the community, at least—against our restoration work. People become more interested in stabilizing the dunes when they think about big destabilizing events."

There, I think as I hang up the phone, is the problem of dune ecosystems and boundary layers in a sentence. To discern the internal structure of a boundary layer, Prandtl had to free his mind from the tyrannies of larger systems. He had to see boundary layers as distinct environments with their own rules, their own behaviors. Along the margins of the northern Pacific Ocean a unique ecosystem, populated with plants that have evolved together over millions of years, clings to life at the interface of land and ocean. To see this boundary ecosystem for what it is, we have to treat it as more than just an appendage to the larger systems that border it. To pry out its secrets, learn its subtleties, takes attention and time. To make people value its presence takes even more time.

Time, though, is what biologists such as Danielle and Andrea may not have. While they struggle to convince us that a sensitive ecosystem needs a little protection from a large human threat, the crustal clock ticks away. The endangered dune plant communities face a greater threat than escalating human intrusions. Before them loom events that will leave them hanging by their cellulose fingernails. They have weathered the big events before. But will they make it through the next cycle? The added stress from human intrusions may be too much, even for a genetic intelligence that evolved within one of the planet's most dynamic boundary layers.

Travel and society polish one, but then a rolling stone gathers
no moss, and a little moss is a good thing on a man.
— John Burroughs, Journal, November 18, 1877

∾

Moss Man

On an August morning I catch the early ferry to the British Columbia mainland. I'm meeting up with the bryologist Terry McIntosh, an expert on the province's mosses. Terry's battered red car is waiting for me when I walk off the boat.

On the road out of the Tsawwassen terminal, our conversation wanders to Wilf Schofield, Terry's adviser when he did his PhD in the 1980s. Schofield, a University of British Columbia professor, was the dominant figure in Pacific Northwest mosses for almost five decades. He mentored several generations of graduate students. I met Schofield in 2008, when I attended a moss workshop he gave. The workshop, as it turned out, was his last class. He died the next month.

I ask Terry what it was like to be one of Schofield's graduate students. "Some professors pull students into their own projects and give them pieces of their projects for student research. Wilf let his students pursue their own interests. He wasn't uninvolved, though. When I decided to work on dryland mosses, a subject about which he knew very little, I had to struggle to convince him that there were enough mosses out there to work on. When I started bringing back mosses that had never been found in the province, he became more enthusiastic."

"Did Schofield help his students find teaching positions in bryology?"

"There are never many positions in bryology. But no, he didn't help much, even for the few positions that came open. His attitude was that your career was *your* career. After my studies at the University of British Columbia, I headed back to my home territory, Ontario, and took a position at Wilfrid Laurier University that had nothing to do with mosses. For the first year, I taught human anatomy and physiology for someone who was on leave. Then I took over part of the introductory biology curriculum and started up a biogeography course. I hardly looked at a moss until I left my university career in the late 1990s and returned to British Columbia."

"Why did you leave?"

"I got tired of school. Even when you are at the top of the academic ladder, it's just school."

Terry negotiates the crazy Vancouver rush hour traffic, braking and accelerating, all the while carrying on a running conversation with me, kibitzing other drivers, and whistling tuneless snippets. The trip might be safer, I decide, with one less distraction. I stop talking and flip open a copy of the resume that Terry sent me. He has his fingers in an astounding number of pies, most of them related in some way to mosses. He's an editor and board member of the Flora of North America project that is publishing the definitive reference volumes on North American mosses. Terry has also done a number of moss reports for COSEWIC (Committee on the Status of Endangered Wildlife in Canada) to help them identify the Canadian mosses that need legal protection. I see on the resume that he has also taken on a large number of contracts with governments and private businesses, mostly to do environmental assessments. When Terry stops for a light, I wave the resume toward him. "You can make a living with all of this?" He laughs. "Yes, believe it or not. My needs are moderate. The biggest problem is getting paid for contracts I've already finished."

On the way to Terry's place, we stop at a small grocery outlet to pick up lunch fixings. While in the store, he strikes up a long conversation with a woman he has never met. Terry seems to lack the filters of propriety that guide most of us. He has the ability to look people in the eye and chat about the most mundane topics—a trait, Annie Dillard once noted, that "one finds among the world's most sophisticated people . . . and also among the world's most unsophisticated people."

We arrive at Terry's apartment. As we climb from the car, Terry points out the dark bands on the bottoms of the boulevard trees along his street. "That's the DPZ," he says. "The Dog Pee Zone. The documentation of the DPZ has been one my major research projects." I think he is kidding, but I can't tell.

Terry, I'm beginning to think, may belong to the unsophisticated branch of Dillard's dichotomy.

∾

Biologists who work in the temperate zones of the globe often qualify their biodiversity estimates by saying "the number of species in this species group is far higher in the tropics than it is here." Bryologists, however, don't have to make this cavil. The earth's temperate regions, it turns out, are lush with moss species. Northern temperate regions that lie next to large oceans, places such as Great Britain, Japan, and the Pacific Northwest, have the greatest variety. British Columbia, Washington, Oregon, and Northern California are a moss Eden.

The abundance of mosses in the Pacific Northwest doesn't mean that mosses are well known to those who live here. Many local naturalists, even those who can identify every plant and bird, are hard-pressed to put names to more than a few of the mosses. This blind spot in the natural history community surprised me when I first moved to British Columbia. Granted, the various species of moss may be more difficult to recognize than species of vascular plants, birds, and mushrooms. But are they that much more difficult? The root of moss neglect, I suspect, lies more in habit than hindrance. We learn from others what we are supposed to see on a walk in the woods. Those we learn from often take their cues from the attention given to a topic by the academic teams that trained them. Botany, unfortunately, has been slow to take into account what some researchers have begun to call the *bryosphere*, the sector of the stegnon boundary layer that is dominated by mosses, liverworts, and hornworts.

The bias in the animal kingdom toward vertebrates—the great majority of animal conservation publications are about vertebrates, even though only one in twenty animal species are vertebrates—has its analogy in the plant kingdom. Vascular plants get an unfair share of academic attention, even in regions where bryophytes play significant roles.

Science has given names, so far, to about ten thousand species of moss. Checklists in British Columbia mention about eight hundred mosses. California has six hundred or so mosses. Washington and Oregon each have some five hundred species. We wouldn't be far off the mark, then, to say that 10 percent of the world's moss species can be found in the Pacific Northwest. Some of these species are dead common. On almost any walk through a forest area on Southern Vancouver Island, we can come across the feathery shoots of *Kindbergia oregana*, Oregon beaked moss. In Washington forests I've seen endless carpets of red stem moss, *Pleurozium schreberi*, in similar habitats. Even our cities are full of moss. The

Kindbergia oregana,
Oregon beaked moss,
a common denizen of
Southern Vancouver
Island forests.

sidewalk cracks in Seattle and Vancouver are chockablock with thread moss, *Bryum argenteum*, as are many of the world's cities. Thread moss, says one moss authority, may be "the most widespread plant on the planet."

If we pull up a clump of one of these common mosses, we notice that the bottom part of the clump is packed with damp, decaying strands. The strands look a bit like roots. Botanists call these lower strands *rhizoids* in order to distinguish them from roots. True roots pick up nutrients and water from the soil and move them, via the plant's circulatory system, into the central stem and upward to the leaves. Mosses, in contrast, do not need to absorb water and shuffle it around inside the plant. Their rhizoids act mostly as anchors and water buffers.

The moss clump we have picked up, closer inspection shows, is composed of many individual plants. With a little teasing we can extract an individual plant. In some mosses, the stem of the plant is firm and unbranched. These mosses, when they put up the reproductive shafts called *sporophytes*, host them on the crown of the growing plant. A clump of these mosses tends to form a tight tuft. Other mosses have flexible, branched stems that bend over and lay along the ground. Sporophytes in these mosses usually emerge from the sides of the moss strands. Mosses of this type form loose mats on tree trunks, logs, and soil. At the top of the sporophyte is a capsule, often no bigger than a grain of rice, that can contain hundreds of thousands of the microscopic spores that give rise to new mosses.

If we scooped up our tuft or mat of moss in wet weather, we would probably find it wearing some shade of green. During the dryer Pacific Northwest summers, mosses often lose their lustrous green colors. Mosses in this dried-out state can seem to be dead. They are not, though—they are just dormant, waiting for wetter weather. When the rains come, mosses recover with amazing speed. Many return to full metabolic activity within an hour of rewetting.

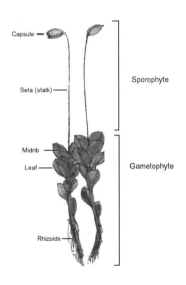

Two stems of a generic moss showing some of the plant parts.

Laboratory tests show that the bulk of the forest mosses operate at full tilt when they are around fifteen degrees Celsius, when the light intensity is about a third of direct sun, and when they are damp but not waterlogged. All of these conditions—cooler temps, partial light, damp substrates—correspond to what we find on forest floors in the Pacific Northwest. Small wonder that residents here find so much moss under their feet.

A closer inspection of the individual plants we have picked out of our clump may reveal male and female sexual structures. These can be quite hard to see. If they are even there. While the majority of mosses do sexual reproduction, a number of them have come to rely, partly or exclusively, on vegetative reproduction. Broken off pieces of almost any moss can make a new plant if embedded in the right growth medium. Moss gardeners take advantage of this kind of reproduction by tossing clumps of mosses into a blender with buttermilk or glue. They paint the chopped-up slurry onto wood or rock and end up, after a few months, with a lush mantle of mosses.

The mosses that manage to reproduce sexually carry it off in an odd way. The curious twists and turns of the moss sexual reproductive cycle bedeviled early research on the small plants. At the beginning of botany's golden age, mosses were thought to have no reproductive structures at all. Johann Jacob Dillenius, an older contemporary of Linnaeus, was convinced that mosses reproduced sexually. He identified the erect sporophytes of mosses, however, as stamens, the male reproductive structures on vascular plants. Linnaeus adopted Dillenius's speculations and carried the confusion forward. At the end of the eighteenth century, a German botanist, Johann Hedwig, put the moss life cycle on firmer footing. He rejected the idea that erect equaled male and made the correct connection between the sporophytes and the female bits. Like the vascular plants, he noted, the male and female parts were sometimes on separate plants, sometimes on the same plant.

Hedwig's investigations brought moss reproduction into a space that plant researchers found comfortable. Mosses now had sexual parts that could be set in correspondence to the ovaries and stamens of the higher plants. When scientists began to take a more genetic perspective on plants at the end of the nineteenth century, however, the correspondences began to break down. The green mosses that we see in the forest, botanists began to realize, were the life stage that corresponds to the reproductive phase in animals and vascular plants. Moss stems and leaves, like our eggs and sperm cells, have only half the full complement of genetic material. The short-lived sporophytes of the mosses, whose cells have sets of paired genes, match up with the stage in which animals and vascular plants spend most of their lives. The sexual life cycle of mosses is, we might say, a mirror image of the pattern in animals and higher plants. Which of these two approaches is the better strategy has been debated, but the point should not be put to a vote. The earliest mosses appeared on earth a half billion years ago—the first plants, some speculate, to have adapted to land—and they continue to thrive today. Big-brained primates, here only a few million years, are not likely to win a genetic pissing match with a group of species that has had a successful five-hundred-million-year run.

But back to that clump of moss we picked up. If we examine the green section of the single strand of moss that we teased from the clump, we notice that it has a stem and leaves. If we put the moss leaves under a microscope, however, we see that they are quite different than the stems and leaves of vascular plants. Moss leaves have no veins, though some have a prominent midrib. The leaf tissue surrounding the moss midrib, moreover, is only one or two cells thick, so moss leaves do not need *stomata*, the holes plants use to breathe in carbon dioxide and breathe out oxygen. Instead of *petioles*, the stalks that typically attach tree leaves to their twigs, the bases of the moss leaves join the stem directly. The differences between plant leaves and moss leaves reflect the more basic differences in plant and moss vascular tissue. In order to pick up the water and nutrients that they need, mosses must find ways to expose the bulk of their cells to moisture-laden air.

When we're finished looking at the clump of moss, we can put it back where we found it—we pulled no roots from the ground when we picked it up. If we were lucky, the brief examination we gave this clump and its stems has revealed what species of moss we found. Some species are easy to recognize, even without a hand lens. To match up the less obvious mosses with what botanists think is the taxonomical scheme represented by these plants, however, we may have to dig into the literature, work through binary keys, and spend long hours peering through dissecting and compound microscopes. Even if we are successful in finding out what moss we have been looking at, we still have in front of us questions that taxonomy cannot answer: What roles do the various species of moss play in the ecosystems that support them? What are mosses *for*?

∾

Terry nabs the bag of groceries from the back seat of the car, and we start the climb to his top-floor apartment, wending our way through a maze of boxes on the treads and landings. Terry announces, as he sorts through the keys on his key ring, that we will drive after lunch to Cypress Provincial Park in the mountains above Vancouver. He unlocks the door and in the narrow hallway we are greeted by a delegation of cats. Terry introduces them and tries to explain how the cats—Ulysses, Zeus, Odin, and Billy—came into his life, but I'm soon lost in a confusion of cat names and cat histories.

At one end of the apartment, a glass door leads out onto a flat roof. I follow Terry through the door and into what appears to be a third-storey garden. At least a hundred pots and planting boxes surround a small hothouse. Here and there I recognize a few garden vegetables. Most of the containers, though, hold native plants. Tucked around the bases of the plants are a variety of mosses. Terry begins to rattle off the scientific names of the plants and mosses and to tell stories about how he acquired the individual plants. One of the mosses he shows me, *Bartramia stricta*, rigid apple moss, is rare. I have read Terry's COSEWIC report on it, but I have yet to find it in the wild. A number of the roof boxes hold clumps of sphagnum mosses. At the end of the tour we squeeze into the hothouse to look at his thirty-year collection of exotic succulents. "My friends know I collect these," he says. "They bring me specimens from all over the world."

Back inside, Terry starts to fix the sandwiches and I wander through the apartment. Cardboard boxes filled

Boxes of moss specimens awaiting further study.

with packets of dried moss are everywhere. Along one wall of his tiny bedroom, I count fifty boxes cantilevered over small shelving boards. If the Big One hits Vancouver at night, the emergency crews will be digging Terry out of a mound of cardboard and dried plants.

In the living room/study, I browse the titles of Terry's library of biology and moss books. He has the volume on antarctic mosses that came out in 2008. I leaf through it. Antarctica is a legend among bryologists. Except for a pearlwort and a hairgrass, Antarctica has no native higher plants. On the 2 percent of the continent that is not locked in ice, lichens and the hundred-plus native mosses have the run of the place. Few bryologists will ever walk the cold moss fields of Antarctica, but just the thought of a continent where mosses are not footnotes sends a shiver of excitement through their spines.

Next to the bookshelf are Terry's dissecting and compound microscopes. The scopes perch on stacks of biology books that aren't about mosses. In the stack of books under the microscope, I spot a metaphor waiting to be harvested. Some of Terry's interests, like his inaccessible books, have been subsumed to his research in bryology. What would my own library show about me, I wonder? Perhaps an obsession with metaphors?

Under the microscope: the fate of biology books that are not about mosses.

The sandwiches are ready and we look around for a place to sit down and eat. Anything like a table has long ago disappeared under lab equipment and moss collections. Terry moves some books and papers to make a place on the sofa. We plump into the soft cushions. "Have you always been interested in plants?" I ask.

"I was an undergrad in college before I fell in love with plants. But I was infatuated with nature even earlier. I had the usual schoolboy chrysalis-in-a-jar that I watched turn into a monarch butterfly. What really triggered my interest in botany, though, was a summer camp. Some friends of mine in Ontario—I grew up in Stratford—were staff members at Silver Lake Mennonite Camp. They persuaded me to become the camp naturalist. I got a copy of the Peterson field guide to plants and started identifying what I could."

Silver Lake Camp. I know the place. For the next few minutes, Terry and I play a game that Mennonites often play when they meet for the first time. The rules of the game require contestants to exchange names of relatives and friends to find out how they are related and how many people they know in common. I've been an eavesdropper at some of these naming events. The shared lists can be huge. Neither of us are Mennonites, but we've both lived around Mennonite communities long enough to be able to play a limited version of the game. We soon discover that there are a half dozen Ontario Mennonites that we both know. Terry wins the game by revealing that he had been married to a Mennonite. I try to counter by proving that I know a cousin of his ex, but we both know it's a feeble gambit. In the Mennonite Game, marriage and blood trump other social relationships.

"You like to win at games, don't you?" I ask.

"It's my ADHD. I've had ADHD all my life, but I didn't know it until last year when I consulted a doctor about a bad depression. Knowing about ADHD helped me to understand a lot of the problems I've had to face. Like other ADHDers, I have too many threads of activity in my life. Sometimes it's hard to know what to work on."

"Medication can help some people with ADHD."

"I know. But I don't take anything. I'd lose the lows, but I'd also lose the highs. The depression worked itself out. One day I went into a coffee shop and found myself smiling and whistling. I stopped a stranger in the shop and said to him 'Hey! I got my mojo back!'"

I think how lucky I was not to be that stranger. We dump our plates in the sink, gather up our gear and mojos, and head out to see the mosses of Cypress Provincial Park.

∾

The winds of the world are not well behaved inside the planetary boundary layer. Above the boundary layer, winds are classical liquids that flow around the globe in rivers of air. Where they skim the surface of the planet, the smooth flows of air become turbulent. The air in these lower layers responds to the rumpled skin of the earth in the same way that a river swirls around rocks poking up from its bed. The closer we get to the ground, as we noted earlier, the more confused the winds.

The earth's plants reside inside the atmosphere's boundary layer, and most plants take advantage, in one way or another, of the interrupted movements of air found in these regions. Certain species of plants, however, are highly attuned to boundary conditions. To see these attuned plants, we need to listen to Prandtl and look down. The narrow band where we find the most condensed changes in wind speed is at our feet, in the stegnon.

Plants that live in the first few centimeters above the surface of the planet are arguably the earth's most typical vegetation. Areas of the globe in which low plants dominate—our grasslands, savannahs, and tundra—occupy as much of the earth's land area as its forests. Even in the world's forested regions with their tall and imposing trees, the low plants that blanket the ground play significant roles. In the mostly treed Pacific Northwest, mosses are a major component of this ground-level vegetation. In some low-light areas in the deep forest, mosses are the only ground plants.

Mosses clue us in to the location of an important subboundary inside the planetary boundary layer: the upper edge of the layer defined by negligible wind speeds. This is normally an invisible line, but where mosses are abundant the line is traced with a pen of green. This boundary is not the same height everywhere. On the floor of a mature stand of trees, the line defined by the tops of mosses can be several centimeters above the ground. On exposed rock balds, the moss mats are much thinner and the line is closer to the ground. Though the green tops of the mosses sketch for us the edges of a boundary layer, mosses do not always draw inside the lines. Many species of moss, for example, jab their sporophytes into the region above the line, taking advantage of the increase in wind speed above the boundary line to disperse their spores.

Over the millennia, mosses have learned to exploit the air movements in the lowest stratum of the planetary boundary layer. Wind, as we know, has a drying effect. It liberates volatile molecules of water from their substrates. On hot days, humans and other mammals seek out places where air moves so that the wind, by pulling away sweat, can cool through evaporation. Mosses, in contrast, prefer not to have their water molecules pulled away. They need them to keep their photosynthetic pathways flowing. But they do like the water and air to circulate. Their solution to the problem is to take up residence in a place where air movements are more gentle. Plants near the ground, where the horizontal air speed is near zero, can take advantage of the vertical turbulence of the wind without the disadvantages of its horizontal drying effect. The water vapor that distills from land warmed by the sun rises and surrounds the stems and leaves of moss. As the air loses its heat at night, the tops of the plants cool. The rising vapor condenses on the top leaves of the plants. Clustered water molecules form heavier-than-air droplets, which detach and plop onto the leaves below. We call this dew. In the diminutive forests of moss, it is a nourishing rain.

The microclimates of the bryosphere attract visitors. A number of insects spend parts of their life cycles in the mosses. Aphids, mites, crane flies, moths, grasshoppers, and midges can often be found sheltering there. Microscopic animals—amoebae, water bears, nematode worms—thrive in the miniature forests. Mosses also provide a moist habitat for slugs and snails. Here in the Pacific Northwest, some ten kilos of banana slugs, one or two thousand of them, pack into every acre of moss-draped forests. The slugs annually crank out their own weight in fecal matter to replenish the thin soils.

More than just animals find homes in the moss. The bryophytes encourage and protect the seeds and young seedlings of some vascular plants and discourage those of others. The water-loving hyphae of fungi huddle in the damp, protected soils under the mosses. Half of all liverworts, the stegnon cousins of the mosses, form direct symbiotic relationships with these fungi.

If we think about mosses only in terms of their immediate contributions to the animals, plants, and fungi that use them, however, we can overlook the larger role that mosses have in maintaining ecosystems and their complex webs of life. Mosses play an important part in water and nutrient cycles. Research carried out by Nalini Nadkarni and her associates in the mountain forest canopies of Costa Rica has shown that forest epiphytes—mostly mosses—can make up a third of the plant biomass. The water storage capacity of the mosses in some forests is equal to that of the tree canopy. The mineral capital banked in the mosses can be two-thirds of what is in tree leaves. To come up with numbers such as these, Nadkarni and other scientists employ sensitive instruments and make measurements over many years, but we can see the ecosystem effects with our own eyes by standing in a moss-draped forest during a heavy rain. The area under the canopy of a bigleaf maple remains relatively dry as the tree's leaves shunt the initial sheets of water to the outer edge of the canopy. Some of the water that eventually seeps into the canopy falls on branches and runs along the wood and down the trunk as *stemflow*. When the stemflow water encounters the mosses that sheath the branches and trunk of the maple, the mosses absorb some of the water. The saturated mosses, acting as miniature reservoirs, pulse out nutrient-charged water in the hours and days after a rain has stopped.

☙

There is still much that we do not know about the role of mosses in Pacific Northwest ecosystems. At the root of our lack of perspective lies a personnel problem. Bryologists are endangered species, and not enough general botanists know the mosses. The problem is worldwide, but the gap stands out in high relief in British Columbia. When Wilf Schofield retired from the University of British Columbia in 1992, he was not replaced with a bryologist. We didn't feel the immediate effect of the university's decision because Schofield had an active postretirement career. Now he's gone and not a single university-level BC academic lists bryophytes as a main area of interest—bold irony in a land described in a 1929 publication as "the bryologist's paradise." It is an Eden without an Adam or Eve.

On the way to Cypress, Terry and I count up the people in Western Canada working on mosses. Alberta, which has about half as many mosses as British Columbia, has at least two professors and a number of graduate students specializing in mosses. We tick through a list of Schofield's graduate students. Those who are doing bryology full time are not in the province; those that are no longer work full-time on mosses. Terry has been picking up some of the slack by mentoring young researchers with an interest in mosses, but it is a small patch on a gaping rip.

Terry's subcompact swerves through the switchbacks leading us up the North Shore Mountains. We have occasional views to the south over the delta of the Fraser River and beyond the delta to Mount Baker. Traffic up here is light, but not long ago this was a busy road—the peaks of Cypress Provincial Park were the snowboarding and cross-country skiing venues for the 2010 Winter Olympics. Even in non-Olympic winters, Cypress is a honeypot for winter sport enthusiasts. Today, though, the parking lot is nearly empty. At a trail map mounted on a wooden kiosk, we plot out the afternoon's walk. No time today for the more strenuous peak hikes. We decide on the short loop to Yew Lake. After a detour around some confusing construction, we find the sign for the trailhead and start on our walk.

This is August. If we were below, in Vancouver and its suburbs, we wouldn't expect to see mosses in their prime, but mountains tend to get more rain. The forest floor mosses are showing well today. As we walk along the well-maintained trail, Terry ticks off the names of the mosses and plants. We pause for closer looks, but not for long—Terry is angling for some mountain bogs halfway up the trail. We soon we step out of the forest and into a small, open valley. Here and there shore pines and hemlocks are eking out a living on tussocks, but most of the valley is a flooded bog. Water draining from the surrounding peaks gets trapped here in shallow stony bowls. The green swatches stretched out before us are the living crowns, says Terry, of at least a dozen different species of sphagnum moss.

Sphagnums are major players in some of the planet's largest unspoiled ecosystems. About 1 percent of the earth's surface, 3 percent of its land area, is covered by sphagnum bogs. The majority of these moss beds lie in a circumpolar belt above the boreal forests of the Northern Hemisphere. Except for a small number of these boggy areas—those in which humans burn dried sphagnum for energy or those in which bogs have been drained for high-latitude agriculture—the sphagnum ecosystems of the Northern Hemisphere are largely intact.

In the Pacific Northwest, which lies mostly to the south of the boreal and hyperboreal belts of sphagnum, we often have to climb, as we have done today, to find large beds of sphagnum. Terry points out *Sphagnum capillifolium* and *Sphagnum papillosum*, two bog mosses that are relatively easy to identify on sight. At another clump of sphagnum he stoops and pulls up a few plants. Peering over his glasses, Terry pinches off the top of the plant head and starts to peel away leaves. "I'm looking at stem leaves," he explains. "The shapes of the leaves near the stem can often tell us the

Terry McIntosh examines a sphagnum moss stem. Photo by Dawn Hanna.

name of the species." He hands the plant to me. The stem leaves are tiny—I have to use a magnifying lens to see them. I flip the plant over. Toward the base there are no rhizoids, just clumps of leaves that are less and less green the farther they are from the top of the plant. The plant has been snapped off. Its rhizoids, if they still exist, were left at the bottom of the bog. Chances are, however, that the march of time has turned the lower bits of this moss strand into pickled peat. Some botanists think that individual sphagnum plants, growing on one end and decaying on the other, can live for thousands of years. As the water level rises or the plants sink into the bog, the long-lived sphagnum stems put up new crowns of leaves to gather sunlight. The leaf cells in the clumps that are below the level that light can reach lose their chlorophyll and die. In some sphagnums these dead cells can absorb twenty times their dry weight in water. The ability of sphagnum to retain water has made it a useful plant. During World War I, a number of factories were set up to make bandages from dried bog moss. Some First Nations peoples used sphagnum clumps as diapers and sanitary napkins.

After an hour we leave the boggy area and continue along the path. As we curve back toward the parking lot, we come across three older adults swimming in one of the tarns. We shout a greeting at them and keep going. Terry, remembering something he wants to ask them, turns back and strikes up a conversation. The swimmers climb from the lake to talk with Terry. Thankfully, they are wearing bathing suits.

We finish the Yew Lake loop and arrive at the parking lot. I volunteer to take a bus back to the ferry, but Terry says he will drive me to the terminal after a quick detour by his house. The Vancouver afternoon traffic is at its max, and Terry's jalopy has no air conditioning, so we are hot and thirsty by the time we emerge from the downtown core. When we get near Terry's house, he says he wants to make a stop at a vet's office to visit another cat that he wants to adopt. Terry goes in to check on the cat while I look over some of the dried mosses on the rocks and try to quench my thirst with Himalayan blackberries. Terry soon joins me, but before he can start to tell me about these city mosses he spots a car with a young boy sleeping in a child seat. The window beside the boy is rolled down a couple of centimeters. Terry goes over to the car and feels the roof. "This is too hot. He needs more air." I wait again while Terry goes into a nearby medical clinic to find the parent. In a few minutes he returns with a not-entirely-pleased mother at his heels.

I point out the time. We need to hurry if I'm going to catch the ferry. We race to the terminal. On the way there, Terry, for the first time today, has nothing to say. In the silence, the metaphor machine in my head cranks away. The fellow driving this car, it seems to me, is what a moss would be if it were a person. He survives on the edge of the world's economic winds, out of the gales of recognizable professional careers, family life, and home ownership, storing and buffering the intermittent stemflows of knowledge that seep through academic botany. He interacts with the slugs and bugs of the forest floor, the people that convention tells us to ignore. Terry's social bryosphere is as foreign to the people in the Pacific Northwest as the region's moss ecosystems are to the majority of its botanists.

I like him, perhaps for the same reason I like mosses.

Mushrooms in brine, for winter eating
— A. S. Pushkin, *Eugene Onegin*

∾

What Does It *Mean?*

A late September rain came down in heavy bursts yesterday, marking the end of another dry Southern Vancouver Island summer. This morning I drove to a forest a few kilometers from my rural home.

On the way to the top of a hill, I push through bushes that only a few weeks ago were heavy with the bounty of late summer: salal berries, huckleberries, blackberries. Red-breasted nuthatches, recently come down from their inland nesting areas, make the woods ring with nasal taunts. Near the summit, I plop down on a bed of *Leucolepis*, tree moss, and lean back against the fallen bole of a forest giant. The scene in front of me is dominated by a stand of second growth Douglas-fir.

What I'm looking for in the forest today is a line, a boundary, between two kingdoms. One of these kingdoms, kingdom Plantae, is represented by the trees, shrubs, and grasses. A second, kingdom Fungi, is the domain of mushrooms, mildews, and molds. Because this second kingdom tends to be less visible than the first, it gets the short end of the attention stick. A century ago the fungi were thought to be nothing more than peculiar plants. If they were covered in a biology curriculum, they were relegated to small weeklong sections of botany courses. Taxonomists liberated them from subservience to plant science in the middle of the

A Southern Vancouver Island forest scene.

twentieth century, transferring them to their own kingdom. In recent decades, kingdom Fungi has wandered even further from kingdom Plantae. Biochemists now suggest that fungi may be more closely related to animals than to plants.

Assigning fungi to their own kingdom has not erased their centuries of vassalage, however. My view of the scene in front of me this morning is still largely phytocentric, focused on members of the plant kingdom. A more mycocentric, mushroom-oriented view would grant the fungi an equal partnership with the plants and animals in this ecosystem. It's a point of view that I find hard to assume this morning. A month from now, though, mushroom caps will begin to dot the ground between the trunks of the trees and the fungi of these woods will be more front and center than they are today.

Next month's mushrooms will testify to the presence of fungi, but the caps are just reproductive bodies. The core of the mushroom is its *mycelium*, which is made up of a matrix of microscopic threads, called *hyphae*. If the minerals and plants and animals and bacteria could be subtracted from the scene in front of me, I would see a gossamer, polychrome world.

The outlines of the trees would still be there, sketched in the finest of lines. Between me and the rocks below would be a fuzzy hyphal pillow. A pointillist haze of fine dust, fungal spores waiting their chance to bud and grow, would replace the soil surface.

We can think about plants and fungi as two large systems of regularity, each with their own rules. They can be—often are—studied in isolation. Plant biologists can ramble on for a long time without mentioning fungi. Mycology textbooks give short shrift to vascular plants. But since the roots of the plants occupy the same region as the fungi and interact with them, somewhere must be a boundary layer, a place of flux where the broad regularities that belong to the two kingdoms break down and new rules appear.

The place to begin looking for the boundary layer between plants and fungi is in the known associations between members of the two kingdoms. During the hundreds of millions of years that they have evolved together, plants and fungi have negotiated a number of deep partnerships. The most commonly cited association assigns to fungi the role of decomposers. Fungal hyphae break down the tissues of dead plants and animals and extract energy and nutrients from this dead matter to carry on their lives. This relationship, as partnerships go, is less than intimate. The plant has to die before the fungus can digest it. To the fungal rotters, trees are rich uncles that leave them a fortune in energy and nutrients when they die.

The decomposer association, however, is only one thread in the story of kingdom cooperation. Many fungi live in full symbiosis with plants. Almost all plants get the energy they need to live and grow directly from the sun. Their cells contain light-absorbing compounds that split hydrogen atoms from their water molecules and join them to carbon dioxide in order to construct the carbon compounds that are the building blocks of life. Fungi, which do not have this ability to turn sunlight into building materials, link up with plants and tap into the plants' supplies of hydrogenated carbon. The plants that live in symbiosis with fungal partners are generous with their carbon, tithing and even double-tithing their net production in order to support their fungal associates. These fungal partners, in their turn, expose the plants to sources of water and nutrients that the plants could never reach on their own. Suzanne Simard at the University of British Columbia has calculated that fungi expand the surface area of some root systems sixty-fold. The minute fungal hyphae, wedging into spaces too small for root hairs to reach, shuffle a steady supply of water and mineral nutrients to the host plant. To acquire these trade goods, enzymes in the hyphae plunder organic deposits in the duff and soil. Fungi also apply acid and hydraulic pressure to break down the soil's composite minerals. In their search for nutrient sources, some fungi even resort to predation. Soil ecologists have discovered that springtails, which often feed on fungi, drop dead when they dine on *Laccaria bicolor*, a symbiotic companion of local conifers. The *Laccaria* mycelium absorbs the nitrogen from the dead insects and passes it along to the conifers.

We have, then, two large, stable systems, the plants and the fungi, and between them a boundary layer, a no-man's-land where the rules of life as a plant and the rules of life as a fungus are compromised and melded. To find this layer, I lean over and turn up a patch of ground next to me. Yesterday's heavy rain has not penetrated far, and I'm soon clawing through a lace of dry roots. I pull up a clump of soil and focus a hand lens on it. Here are the telltale signs of the boundary layer: blunt plant rootlets covered with what looks like tightly wound gauze bandages. I put my nose into the hole I have dug. The smell of mold and mushroom is strong.

Fungal mantles on the root tip and lateral roots of a western hemlock. Photo by Marty Kranabetter. Reproduced with permission from the NRC Research Press publication R. Larry Peterson et al., Mycorrhizas: Anatomy and Cell Biology Images *(2006).*

More than 90 percent of vascular plant species, scientists now think, live in these carbon-for-nutrient symbioses with fungi. We refer to the fungi in these relationships as *mycorrhizal* (mushroom/root) fungi. In the forest before me there are two important types of mycorrhizas. The oldest of these connections between host plants and fungi, the ones that mycologists call *arbuscular* mycorrhizas (AMs), are named for arbuscules, the treelike branchings of the fungal hyphae inside the root cells of plants. It's an old, old relationship—the large spores typical of AM fungi appear in Silurian fossils laid down 440 million years ago. The earliest exemplars of these fungi, it is now believed, may have appeared on earth a billion years ago. Could a fungal association have enabled photosynthetic water plants to make their first steps onto the soil-free land? The lichenized fungus eking out a living on a bare rock near me suggests that the idea has some merit. I don't see any vascular plants nibbling at the stone.

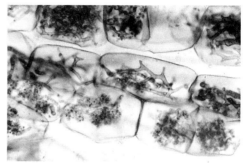

The hyphal coils and arbuscules of an arbuscular mycorrhiza have colonized the cells of a ginseng root. Reproduced with permission from the NRC Research Press publication R. Larry Peterson et al., Mycorrhizas: Anatomy and Cell Biology Images *(2006).*

Because the primitive AM fungi do not usually form visible reproductive bodies, they pass unnoticed to all but botanists and mycologists. They are, however, extremely common: two-thirds of all known species of land plants accept AM symbiosis. It may be that *all* land plants have the genetic disposition to form a partnership with AM fungi and the plants that don't do it have rejected this symbiosis somewhere in their evolutionary careers.

AM fungi can colonize new plants with phenomenal speed. Transplant a new seedling into a location inhabited by the right fungus and hyphae several centimeters away will immediately start to grow toward it. Within two days of contact, the AM fungus will form its first structures on the exterior wall of the plant's root. In less than two weeks after contact, the new plant will be colonized and fungal arbuscules will have taken up residence inside the root cells, turning the AM fungus and its host plant into an almost indissoluble organic unit.

AMs are the mycorrhizas of agricultural plants and species-rich ecosystems. A typical AM partnership would involve a crop growing on lush prairie soil or a fast-growing tree in the tropics. When we think of the mycorrhizal associations of plants in the Pacific Northwest, however, the ones we call *ectomycorrhizas* (EMs)* command more attention. EM plant-fungus associations are much younger than their AM counterparts. They may have arisen in the early Carboniferous, a mere 130 million years ago. And they are less common—fewer than 5 percent of modern plant species form these EM connections. Comparing percentages, however, is misleading, especially in ecosystems such as the one in front of me today. The relative importance of the EM associations is magnified by the types of plants and the amount of the earth's surface occupied by these plants. Trees in the pine, oak/beech, birch/alder, and willow families—the kinds of trees that predominate in the Pacific Northwest—seem to prefer EM partnerships.

To the botanist, three features signal an EM-colonized plant. The first is a mantle, a sheath of hyphae, around sections of the plant root. These are the gauze bandages on the root tips that I pulled from the soil. In some cases, EM fungi envelop almost all of the root tips of their symbiotic partners, replacing the tree's own root hairs. The second feature of an EM-colonized plant is a network of fungal hyphae that reaches into areas between the cell walls of the root. To see this net, we would need to look at a cross section of the root under a compound microscope. The third feature of EM-colonized plants is a far-flung net of hyphae that extends from the mantles into the soil around the roots. A single kilogram of soil from a forest like this may contain two hundred kilometers of these fungal strands.

A scanning electron microscope image of an alder root tip that has been colonized by poison pax, an EM mushroom, showing the mantle and some of the hyphae reaching out into the surrounding soil. Reproduced with permission from the NRC Research Press publication R. Larry Peterson et al., Mycorrhizas: Anatomy and Cell Biology Images *(2006).*

---

*"Ecto-" because these mycorrhizas usually do not penetrate the cell walls of the host plant. AMs are endomycorrhizas.

Even when we haven't got the laboratory equipment that we need to detect the three main features of EM colonization, we can still be fairly certain, for at least two or three months of each year, that we are in the presence of EM connections: the fungi that make these connections usually reproduce by shooting up mushrooms around their host plants. At least six thousand different species of mushroom-producing fungi are known to make EM connections with host plants. When we happen on boletes, corts, chanterelles, fiberheads, hedgehogs, russulas, trichs, and amanitas growing around trees and bushes, chances are good that the fungi have EM associations with the nearby plants. A given species of tree may cohabit with thousands of different fungal species, and a single tree, botanists have found, can support ten or more different EM associations at the same time. The Douglas-firs in the forest around me are especially promiscuous when it comes to choosing fungal partners.

Thinking about host plants and their EM and AM fungi as a single unit is a revolutionary idea. But research over the last twenty-five years hints at an even more radical concept. We know that a given mycorrhizal fungus may colonize several plants in the same area, even plants of different species. We have also discovered that the hyphae of compatible mycorrhizas readily fuse into a single, interconnected mesh. Carbon compounds from one photosynthesizing plant can be shunted along the interconnected hyphal strands into neighboring plants. These complex meshes that connect several plants together are called *common mycorrhizal networks* (CMNs).

We can see evidence of ectomycorrhizal CMNs in our Vancouver Island forests. When a tree that is part of a CMN is cut off a meter or so above the root, it doesn't always die. It can persist as a living stump, begging crumbs of carbon and nutrients from the fungal mesh that it once supported. Other clues to the presence of CMNs are the small plants that do not make their own chlorophyll. Several varieties of local plants—indian pipe, pinesap, and the various coralroot orchids—are not, as we once believed, rotters that live directly off the decaying duff of the forest floor. Their roots form mycorrhizal partnerships with russulas and other fungi that are part of CMNs. The carbon and nutrients that these plants require derive from their CMN partners.

Two living stumps of Douglas-fir enjoy the meals provided by a neighboring tree through a common mycorrhizal network.

CMNs threaten to overturn the way we think about the natural world. When a forest ecologist told the late Donella Meadows, one of the authors of *Limits to Growth* and the founder of the Sustainability Institute, about research on CMNs, the revelation stopped her in her tracks. "The trees pass stuff around?" she asked, "What does that *mean*"

We have only begun to put an answer to Meadows's question. At a minimum, CMNs shake up our notions of evolutionary competition and make us rethink forest management. But the study of CMNs may carry us much further in coming decades. The beginning of a new understanding of forest systems—systems like the one I'm in now—is coded in the *woodwide web*, the boundary layer where plants and fungi come together. I think of this new perspective as mycocentric because it redresses an earlier lack of attention to the invisible fungi of these forests. What we are moving toward, however, is a place where we see the outlines of a picture that is neither phytocentric nor mycocentric. It is the *partnership* between the EM fungi and the vascular plants that manages a significant part of the forest budget, sharing out the limited resources, deciding who thrives and who dies.

I lever myself from my seat beside the log and shift my weight to legs gone stiff from the long sit. In a month or so the fungi will put out their mushrooms and we will have a better sense of the partnerships that make this forest work.

∞

The mushroom that I find nestled in a bed of moss is soggy from a week of October rain. A third of it has been eaten by slugs. I dig it up, careful to preserve the base, and peer under the cap. The violet and brown gills hint that it might be a cort, but the remnant of the diaphanous veil that is usually plastered against the upper stem of corts is faint in this specimen. But what else could it be? A blewit? I pass the gills under my nose. They lack the fruity smell of blewit gills. Definitely a cort, the first large cort we have seen this morning.

Oluna is down the hill, twenty paces away. I wade through a dense patch of Oregon grape and show her the mushroom. She takes it from me and turns it over once, twice, in her hands. "Yes," she says, "a *Cortinarius*," the middle syllable of the word taking on the open "ah" sound of her native Czech vowels. I wait for an explanation, expecting a Socratic tutorial showing what I should have noticed about the mushroom and revealing, at the end of a chain of iron logic, the name of the species. Oluna is patient with my poor memory and generous with her lessons, but I have to wonder: Does she really imagine that my brain could be trained to work like hers? She knows mushrooms the way a pathologist knows diseases—in a few seconds her mind makes and rejects more hypotheses than I could conjure in an hour. I try to follow her on these mental dashes, but our trips often end with the remark that I have "fallen off the strawberry." This is a Czech idiom, she says, for missing something really obvious.

This time, though, I don't see the wry smile that precedes one of her tutorials. The specimen I've handed her, either because of its rarity or because it is damaged, defies field identification. To decide which of the thousand species of genus *Cortinarius* I have found, Oluna will need a microscope, some chemical reagents, and access to specialized monographs. She may even have to send part of the mushroom away for DNA analysis. For every hour Oluna spends in the field collecting specimens, she spends another three or four hours in her lab dissecting, drying, and sketching the samples. She sighs and fishes in her bag for a piece of wax paper to wrap the mushroom.

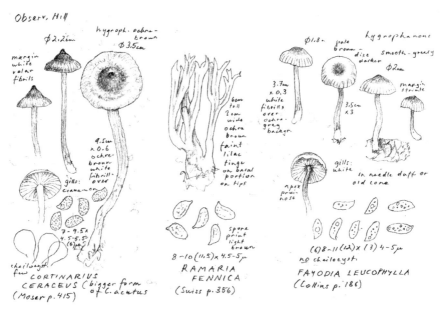

A page from Oluna Ceska's Observatory Hill notebook. Reproduced with permission. Photograph by Adolf Ceska.

Today two of us—I and the botanist Hans Roemer—have joined Adolf and Oluna Ceska to sniff out mushrooms on the north face of Victoria's Observatory Hill. Oluna has been doing fungal surveys on the hill's seventy-odd hectares for more than five years. This enclave of ravines, rock balds, creek beds, and Douglas-fir forest is a government property managed by the Herzberg Institute of Astrophysics. At the top of the two-hundred-meter hill is a pair of telescopes, one of which was, for a few brief months in the early part of the twentieth century, the second largest telescope in the world. The telescopes are still used, though these days the library, dorms, meeting rooms, and public education displays surrounding the observatories attract more people than do the instruments themselves. Biologists often find themselves in opposition to land developers, but the buildings on these grounds are a net gain to botanists and mycologists. The cloak of federal protection, with its restrictions on commercial development, makes Observatory Hill an important locale for researching the natural systems of Southern Vancouver Island. Hans and other botanists have studied the vascular plants on the property. Adolf and Oluna know that they can return year after year to study the mushrooms here without worrying about armies of backhoes ripping up the beds of fungi.

Oluna's surveys of Observatory Hill have turned up more than a thousand different species of mushrooms. Her study is one of only a handful of multiyear science-based inventories of the mushrooms at a single site. An unexpected conclusion that has emerged from these long-term studies is just how misleading short-term inventories can be. In a five-year study, a third or more of the mushrooms that are recorded in a given year will be sightings not found in any other year. What triggers these odd cycles is not well known. Oluna has been able to find some correlation between certain mycorrhizal mushrooms and moisture patterns, but much mystery remains. Because of these sighting inconsistencies, no one knows the real extent of the genetic treasure that presses back against our steps today. To make estimates of the number of fungal species, botanists use a six-to-one rule: for every vascular plant species, they say, we should expect about six fungal species. Hans tells me that Observatory Hill hosts about two hundred species of vascular plants. If the rule holds, Oluna's site inventory may one day put names to about twelve hundred species of mushrooms. My bet is that she will find more.

I met Adolf and Oluna about the time they began their Observatory Hill study, when I showed up at a meeting of the local mushroom club. Mushroom clubs attract people who have many different agendas. A number of the members will be people who like to eat wild mushrooms. Others will enjoy photographing mushrooms. Some, especially those with field naturalist backgrounds, will have an interest in identifying mushrooms. It didn't take long, after I joined the Victoria club, to find out that we had more than a half dozen members who could put a name to most of the local mushrooms. Adolf and Oluna, though, were in a class by themselves, experts to whom the other club experts deferred.

Any foray that mentioned their names would attract dozens of people. Oluna's passion for learning more about mushrooms and her willingness to share what she knows seems to draw others to her.

Oluna Ceska on a Vancouver Island foray.

I've been on a number of Oluna's forays. While people crowd around Oluna and ply her with questions, Adolf and I often wander ahead to scout out some of the less common mushrooms. The discussions that Adolf and I have on these reconnaissance trips sometimes wander away from fungal topics. We talk about the experiences that have brought us to where we are. Even today, with just the four of us, Adolf and I seem to need breaks from the search that Oluna and Hans do not. Adolf tells me that he and Oluna came to British Columbia in 1969, slipping between the fingers of the communist regime that reasserted control over Czechoslovakia in the wake of Alexander Dubček's brief stint as leader of a reformist government. Adolf had grown up in a Czech home that was, he says, "politically incorrect," and he had limited access to the secondary school system. By the early 1960s, he and Oluna had met and married, and both of them had completed the equivalent of a master's degree at Prague's Charles University, Adolf working on vegetation ecology and Oluna on fungi. Oluna took a job as a laboratory scientist for a Czech corporation and Adolf started work on his doctorate in plant ecology. About this time a biologist on sabbatical from the University of Victoria showed up in Prague. The biologist was on the lookout for students who could be drawn into research circles in British Columbia. He snagged Hans Roemer on that trip and later sent an invitation to the Botanical Institute of the Czechoslovak Academy of Sciences that ended up in Adolf's hands. Adolf and Oluna negotiated a two-year stay at the University of Victoria, but the euphoria of the short Prague Spring persuaded them to delay the adventure. The delay nearly canceled their trip. They boarded their flight to Canada a month before the communist puppet government sealed the Czech borders.

The Ceska's connections with their homeland began to unravel once they arrived in Canada. At the end of their second year in British Columbia, they applied to the Czech government for an extension of their stay. Their request was denied. When their visas expired, they were faced with choices that seemed to have only disadvantages. They had not made financial arrangements to stay in Canada for an extended period. But an immediate return to Czechoslovakia also had drawbacks—conditions in their homeland seemed increasingly inhospitable to people of their political bent. They pondered the problem, wrote letters, took counsel. In the end, they decided to stay in Canada, even though it forced them into the limbo of illegal immigrancy. Their failure to return earned them, as they feared, sentences to prison terms in Czechoslovakia. Canada in the meantime took no immediate action to deport them. After a few years they were able to apply for Canadian citizenship.

Breaking ties with their native land meant that Adolf had little hope of finishing the degree he had started in Prague. Oluna had accepted employment, soon after they arrived in Canada, as a research associate with the University of Victoria, a job she would keep for the next twenty-five years. Using Oluna's small salary as their financial base, Adolf started on another PhD program at the University of Victoria. After completing his degree in 1978, he continued to study the wetland vascular plants that he had researched for his doctoral thesis, taking on private contracts to do vegetation surveys. In 1981 he accepted a position at the Royal BC Museum as curator of botany. Field trips that Adolf made in his new job would add thirty-five thousand specimens to the museum's herbarium, and he would author and review a large number of chapters for provincial botany publications. In the last years before his nominal retirement, he moved over to the BC Ministry of the Environment. At the ministry he focused on inventories of rare Vancouver Island plants.

Oluna, meanwhile, was pulled away from her initial interest in fungi by the demands of her research job. She studied metabolic pathways in agricultural plants and authored a series of journal articles on taste- and smell-producing molecules. She also honed her skills as a botanical illustrator. In her spare time, Oluna helped Adolf with his expanding work on vascular plants. Only in the mid 1990s was she able to pick up the threads of her earlier work on fungi. When Adolf retired, he found his own interests wandering toward fungi. This time Oluna took the research lead and Adolf became her assistant.

In the 1990s, with the fall of the communist regimes in Eastern Europe and the emergence of the new Czech Republic, Adolf and Oluna returned to visit family and friends they had left behind in the 1960s. They were finally able to look at the files from the legal proceedings that had led to their absentee prison sentences. Like many who had fled Iron Curtain countries in the postwar decades, they were shocked by the documents they found in their files. Accusations had been written by family members and by people that they had known as friends in their earlier life.

Adolf and I rejoin Hans and Oluna to work the upper part of the Observatory Hill slope. At lunchtime the four of us turn downhill and head to the pull-off where we left our cars. Oluna's list for the day notes about a hundred species of mushrooms. Samples of about half of them are in her collection bag, homework for the next few days.

∾

The science careers of Hans Roemer and the Ceskas have unfolded in a North American landscape. The three of them bring, however, a continental European perspective to their work in botany and mycology. They inhabit, we might say, a kind of intellectual boundary layer. To get their take on what it's like to work in this milieu, I've arranged to meet Adolf, Oluna, and Hans at the My Chosen Cafe, a restaurant in the small community where I live. The café, frequented by visitors from nearby Victoria, is usually crowded. On this rainy afternoon most of the dining rooms are empty. I nab a table beside an open fireplace. By the time Hans, Oluna, and Adolf show up, my damp clothes are steaming.

While we wait for someone to take our orders, I ask Hans how he came to leave his native Germany. His move to Canada, he tells me, had a direct connection to the way that Europeans do plant ecology. When he studied ecology at the Technical University of Hanover, Reinhold Tüxen was his teacher. Tüxen had been one of the earliest students of Josias Braun-Blanquet, the founder of the European schools of plant sociology. Hans became familiar with the methods and techniques of the Braun-Blanquet schools while he was working at Tüxen's private research institute during his university breaks. One of the international visitors to this institute, Marc Bell of the University of Victoria, arrived with an offer of a research assistantship for a student trained in the botanical skills taught in the European schools. Hans took the offer and moved to Victoria to do a PhD in plant ecology as soon as he finished his master's degree in Hanover. At the end of his doctoral work, wanting to continue his research on North American vegetation, Hans and his wife decided to stay on in Canada.

The Braun-Blanquet school that Hans is talking about was, and still is, the dominant force in European plant ecology. Comparisons are made between the significance of Braun-Blanquet's work and the revolutions in botany triggered by Linnaeus and Darwin. In recent decades, the Braun-Blanquet school has divided into several subschools, but all of the schools share a field toolkit. A botanist planning to study a given region with the methods of plant sociology marks out a plot and makes a shorthand summary of all the plant species that occur within the plot. The researcher notes on the summary the coverage, growth patterns, and relative health of the plants in the plot. A similar summary is done for several plots in a region and the various summaries are combined into a single table, with species listed in the left column and plot names in the column headers. The rows and columns of the table are then reordered to give prominence to diagnostic species, the plants that are neither uncommon (occurring rarely or not at all in most plots) nor common (occurring frequently in all plots). The diagnostic species are drawn, when appropriate, from the various vegetation layers—upper canopy trees, mid-level shrubs, and ground-hugging forbs and grasses. The vegetation type for a plot then becomes some version of the names of one or two of the plot's diagnostic species. Plots that have the same vegetation types can be lumped together to define regions with a common ecosystem.

The European revolution in ecosystem studies that is behind this field method has received a cool reception in the United States. The social metaphors employed in Braun-Blanquet's 1928 *Pflanzensoziologie* (published in English as *Plant Sociology* in 1932) may have discouraged its uptake. In the postwar American culture of the 1940s and 1950s, any academic discourse that seemed sympathetic to European traditions of socialism became a target of political suspicion. Canadian botany, however, turned the same friendly face toward the European botanical methods that it did toward European socialism. By the time Hans arrived in Canada, botanists on the West Coast had already started using the Braun-Blanquet methods to divvy up British Columbia into distinct ecosystems.

The person most responsible for importing the European botanical methods into Western Canada was another displaced Czech. Vladimir J. Krajina rose to prominence in his native Czechoslovakia, becoming a docent in botany at Charles University in the 1930s and taking on various administrative positions at the school. When the Nazis overran Czechoslovakia and closed its universities, Krajina joined the resistance movement. He managed to pass along to colleagues in England, via clandestine radio links, thousands of messages about German activities. Eventually arrested by the Nazis, Krajina lived for more than two years under the constant threat of execution. He survived his long imprisonment and after the war returned to his academic career. Promoted to full professor at Charles University, Krajina soon became active in the new Czech political parties. As the secretary-general of a party that opposed the communists, his position became untenable when the USSR tightened its hold on Czechoslovakia. Krajina fled Czechoslovakia in 1948 and moved to British Columbia in 1949. He climbed the same academic ladder in Canada that he had scaled in his homeland during the 1930s. Over the next thirty years, Krajina and his students at the University of British Columbia would use the plant associations defined by the Braun-Blanquet methods to organize the ecosystems of Canada's West Coast.* When Hans arrived in Canada, he became one of Krajina's students, completing a postdoc under him and working closely with him on provincial projects in the 1970s and early 1980s.

I ask Adolf and Oluna if they knew their fellow countryman. "Of course," says Adolf. "The community of Czech botanists in the province is small. But we were kept at a distance. It wasn't until much later, during Krajina's last years, that we learned the reason. Krajina believed that we had been sent over by the Czech communists to spy on him! We had been in Canada almost a decade before we were able to have an open discussion with him."

Hans, who served for many years as the botanist and plant ecologist for British Columbia's network of biological reserves, tells us about some of the field studies he and Krajina did. The reserves they worked to organize were established by the provincial legislation in the 1970s as repositories of rare and unique habitats—no commercial development is permitted on the reserve lands, and individuals and groups use them only for educational and scientific purposes. Krajina's goal was to set aside about 1 percent of British Columbia's land base in these new ecological reserves, a goal he fell short of by a factor of five. Hans and others who have been involved in the creation and extension of the reserves over the last four decades worry about the political retreat from the principles behind the founding of ecological reserves. The reserves, hybrids whose parents are the European tradition of plant ecology and the wilderness preservation movement of the Canadian West, have been orphaned by several changes of provincial regimes.

The waitress arrives and we sort out drinks and food. I ask Hans, Adolf, and Oluna whether mushrooms were important to them when they were growing up. "To a certain degree everyone in Europe is interested in mushrooms," says Oluna. "You have to take into account," Hans adds, "that we grew up when times were hard, the years just after the war. I would go out with my mother and sister to walk through the fields

---

* In the two decades before he died in 1993, Canada and Czechoslovakia conveyed on Krajina all the major awards they could give him. Canada's National Film Board did a documentary on him. In 2012, the first book-length biography appeared (Jan Drabek's *Vladimir Krajina: World War II Hero and Ecology Pioneer*).

and forests between the villages in order to gather food. We would pick mushrooms and steal the odd turnip or potato from the fields. We called it *hamstering*, which means gathering. When things got really bad, we would beg. We'd go up to farmhouses, knock on the door, and ask if the farmer could spare a potato. The adults would stay in the background. If we were feeling really bold, we would ask for an egg."

"You can see the contrast between Canadian and European attitudes toward mushrooms," says Adolf, "when you compare an English writer like Shakespeare to a continental writer like Pushkin. Shakespeare hardly mentions mushrooms. In Pushkin's writings, the women sit around a table preparing mushrooms."

Adolf's comment about Shakespeare and Pushkin, I have learned, reflects a divide in European folkways that runs along the English Channel. The Europeans that most Canadians count as their ancestors, the ones who lived in England, Scotland, Ireland, and Wales, were notorious mycophobes. To them mushrooms were toadstools that had no part in cuisine and medicine. Unlike the markets in European countries, which sell a wide range of seasonal fungi, markets in Britain and North America offered, until recently, only one mushroom.* When the people of the British Isles settled the United States and Canada, they brought their mycophobic attitudes with them.

"Does this difference in attitude have any effect on the how European academics handle mushrooms?" I ask the three botanists.

"I think so," says Adolf. "Europe in general has a healthier relationship between professional and amateur science. Many who have no formal connection to universities are able to work at the cutting edge of research." The conversation around the table veers off into the exceptions, the North Americans that Hans and the Ceskas have worked with who contributed to science without benefit of academic credentials. As I listen to this litany of names and stories, I become aware how the European context from which these three have emerged enables them to

---

Agaricus bisporus, the white button mushroom, is the supermarket staple. Crimini and portobello mushrooms are not exceptions to this one-mushroom rule—they are just varieties of the button mushroom. Like Ford with his black Model T, North American supermarkets will sell customers any mushroom they want, as long as it is *Agaricus bisporus*.

cultivate and encourage a people's science. Amateurs with an interest in the natural systems of Southern Vancouver Island belong to a number of interlinked societies and clubs that are focused on mushrooms, botany, birds, hiking, and native plants. Hans and the Ceskas have contributed their expertise to almost all of these amateur groups. This populist connection was probably not a conscious choice on their part. They didn't decide when they came to Canada that they wanted to hobnob with amateurs—they brought with them from Europe a perspective on science that already included linkages between formal and informal science.

The conversation turns to other differences between European and North American mycology. "Several European countries," I point out, "maintain lists of threatened and endangered species of fungi. Are there also North American lists?"

"Not many," says Adolf, "We ran into this problem of at-risk fungi with a species of mushroom that we found on Observatory Hill. *Squamanita paradoxa* is a rare parasitic fungus. It has been reported from only a few sites around the world. Our discovery was the third collection of the species from the Pacific Northwest. We contacted a mycologist at the University of Washington about this mushroom. He wanted Oluna to write an article describing it. We hesitated—*Squamanita* was just one of a large number of at-risk mushrooms that our work has turned up. This made us think about doing something more extensive on rare mushrooms. I sent an e-mail to conservation centers in several US states where there were important collections of fungal specimens and asked them if lists of at-risk fungi were available. The replies were almost all negative. New York and California, for example, had nothing. Minnesota had a tiny list with about ten species. Oregon had a list, but it was mostly concerned with truffles."

"The national lists of endangered fungi kept by Switzerland and Germany are quite large, aren't they?" I ask.

"Yes," says Adolf. "If we had such lists here, chances are that they would contain many more species than the indexes of endangered vascular plants that we currently maintain." I raise the issue of Canada's national COSEWIC list. In its at-risk categories COSEWIC recognizes about six hundred species. Nearly four hundred items on the list are animals, the other two hundred are plants. Of the plants, 90 percent are

The powdercap strangler (Squamanita paradoxa) *discovered by the Ceskas on Observatory Hill in 2009. The sheath on the bottom of the stems is the remnant of the* Cystoderma *mushroom infected by the strangler. Photograph by Adolf Ceska.*

vascular plants and the rest are mosses and lichens. The list contains no mushrooms. I ask Adolf whether he and Oluna have tried to get COSEWIC to accept a mushroom.

"I offered to do this last year," Adolf says, "for *Tubaria punicea*, the Christmas mushroom that grows at the base of decaying arbutus trees. Oluna had contributed to an article on the mushroom. When I contacted COSEWIC, they said that we were welcome to submit a report on the mushroom, but they guaranteed that it wouldn't be put on the list."

"What I can't understand," Oluna says, "is why Canada allows lichens on their list of endangered species and not fungi. Lichens are fungi with algal partners."

"But *why* doesn't COSEWIC include fungi?" I ask.

Oluna's gray-green eyes flash. A lifetime of being pushed to the margins can generate some anger. "That's the question, isn't it? It's time. How long should we wait?"

"I think," says Hans, "that the proportions on the current COSEWIC list reflect orders of difficulty in doing the descriptions rather than the reality of risk."

"We lack good data on fungi, true," says Oluna, "but we could at least make a start. Getting something on an official list would stimulate the research we need in order to add more."

"Yes," Hans agrees, "it's a negative cycle." We sit and look at our drinks for a while. I'm uncomfortable with the pause, so I break the silence with a joke. Something else that I have noticed about continental Europeans—when a conversation leads to a logical dead end, they often mark it with a longer pause than North Americans can tolerate.

The afternoon's conversations replay in my mind as we leave the café and its warm fire and walk back into the cold drizzle. Following a trail of mushrooms has led me to two boundary layers. The first layer was the one sheltering the mycorrhizal mushrooms at the interface between kingdom Fungi and kingdom Plantae. The second is the one at the Canadian interface between European and North American perspectives on ecosystems.

Boundary layer solutions don't always travel well—what works inside a boundary layer may not work outside it. At times, however, the compromises found through boundary layer experiences can seep out of the narrow regions where they have been discovered and give insight into problems belonging to the larger bounding systems. Our new awareness of mycorrhizal symbioses, for example, may one day revolutionize our understanding of environmental processes. Mycorrhiza researchers have a sense that they are standing at the edge of an intellectual synthesis that will affect the way we look at both plants and fungi. As I watch Hans and the Ceskas splash through the parking lot to their car, I also wonder if the Canadian fusion of European and American botanical traditions might have something to say about topics that vex environmental scientists in the older traditions.

I'd like to learn more about this Canadian boundary layer between European and North American traditions. I know someone—he doesn't live far from here—who can help.

We can never know how wide a circle of disturbance we produce in the harmonies of nature when we throw the smallest pebble into the ocean of organic being.
— George Perkins Marsh, *The Earth as Modified by Human Action* (1874)

Elusive Ecosystems

A few years after it was founded, the Research Branch of British Columbia's Forest Service assembled its ecologists and interns for a group picture. In the picture, which can be seen on the Internet, the men—women had yet to break into the closed ranks of forestry—model the fashions of the 1970s, outfitting themselves in an array of bell-bottoms, plaids, and turtlenecks. Several styles of coifs, mustaches, and beards frame their faces.

Almost everyone in the picture is young. At the time the picture was taken, the timber industry was a significant slice of the BC economy. The provincial government, flush with revenue from its timberlands, decided to spend some of its windfall to find out what ecologists could tell them about forest management. Forest ecology, a relatively new discipline, was expanding rapidly, and governments and forest companies were sweeping in college grads almost as fast as they could be produced.

I've arranged to meet Andy MacKinnon, one of the young men in the photo, at his Metchosin residence. As Andy fixes us cups of tea, his wife Mairi, wrapped in an oversized bathrobe, shuffles into the kitchen and croaks out a greeting. She has picked up the same pneumonia that felled Andy two weeks earlier.

Andy and I carry our cups to the dining/living room. Several of the decorations in their home reflect Andy and Mairi's heritage. Two Scots united, Andy tells me, when the pair of them got together. Andy is a MacKinnon, Mairi a Donaldson. I visualize Andy decked out in a kilt and dropped into some Highlands croft. With his tall frame, ruddy face, and green eyes, he would fit right in. As long as he didn't talk. Living in Canada for several generations has clipped the burr from the MacKinnon speech.

Several Scots, I know, were pioneers in Pacific Northwest botany. I ask Andy if genes have contributed to his interest in ecology. He laughs. "No, I'm the white sheep—or perhaps green sheep—of my clan. The family profession is law. Three generations of my family were called to the bar. I had two grandfathers who were judges. My father and my uncle sat together on the BC Supreme Court. A brother and a sister are lawyers. Many of my fifty-plus first cousins are lawyers. Even my wife is a lawyer!"

"Then how did you end up in the Forest Service?"

"Partly by accident. I did an undergrad degree in botany. Then I did a master's in mycology. There wasn't much demand for mycologists in those days. To do anything with my graduate degree I would have had to stay in school, finish a PhD, and pursue an academic career. In the year that I graduated, the Forest Service was advertising for someone to carry out vegetation mapping in Northeastern BC. I decided I would rather play in the woods than stay in school. The job turned out to be part of the effort to map the province's biogeoclimatic zones."

∾

These *biogeoclimatic zones*, which live at the boundary between European and North American perspectives on natural systems, are what I've come to ask Andy about. The term is not an easy one to understand. Hidden in the phrase is a century of not-always-friendly conflict in the field of ecology.

Ecology is one of the newest sciences. The word *ecology* was coined in the second half of the nineteenth century. Ecology textbooks laid the foundations for an independent field of study in the decades bracketing the turn of the twentieth century. Over the next twenty years researchers labored to launch ecological societies and invent academic programs. By the second third of the twentieth century all the heavy lifting had been done. Ecology had emerged as a mature branch of science, and ecologists assumed a status similar to that of other biological science professionals.

In the family tree of the modern sciences, ecology is pictured as an offspring of biology. Linking biology and ecology as parent and child, however, is misleading. Biology itself has not been around all that long. It only emerged as a distinct academic discipline in the first half of the nineteenth century, when it precipitated out of a broader quest for knowledge known as *natural philosophy*. The early biologists, in order to establish their discipline as an independent science, restricted themselves to topics that could be studied in a laboratory, the sanctuary of science. Subjects that could not be handled with incantations in glass and brass were shunted to the side. The topics deferred by the early biologists included many issues that we now associate with ecology, such as the in situ connections between organisms and the complex roles of these organisms in the natural world. Darwin, a pioneer in the study of the questions that would later be asked by ecologists, laid aside his work on the evolution of species for twenty years while he earned street cred in the new science of biology by authoring a tedious tome on barnacles. Real biology, he and his cohorts believed, required hours of peering through microscopes and dissecting specimens. Darwin's hesitation to publish his thoughts about evolution, recent biographers suggest, was a result of an inner turmoil stirred up by his changing religious outlook. While complex theological and emotional motives may have contributed to the publication delay of his thoughts on evolution, a much simpler explanation suggests itself. The scientific establishment that defined Darwin's career was sifting through the older perspectives of natural philosophy, deciding what did and did not belong to the new discipline of biology. The young Darwin read the writing on the wall and kept silent—until his hand was forced by colleagues with less respect for the rules—about speculations that could not be brought into a laboratory. It was mostly a desire for the approval of his colleagues in the Linnean Society and a shared concern for their young science, not the fear of parsons and priests, that shaped his early career.

By the end of the nineteenth century, biologists had gained more confidence in their discipline and were ready to revisit issues that they had set aside earlier in the century. These recovered topics included, besides evolution, the relationships between organisms that we now associate with ecology. Not everyone was convinced, however, that wider ecological questions could be addressed in a scientific manner. The Ecological Society of America (ESA), home today to many of the world's card-carrying ecologists, was launched in 1915 after the early ecologists failed to convince the Botanical Society of America (BSA) to host an ecology section. These first ecologists faced the same issues of legitimization that their biological predecessors had dealt with a century earlier.

A fledgling science in search of approval from its fellow sciences can't be too careful about the company it keeps. As the decades of the twentieth century passed, ecologists immersed themselves in the details of their research and avoided topics that were linked to explicit philosophical, political, and social agendas. In the 1940s, a cabal of ESA officers tried to restrict the political lobbying activities of the organization's Committee for the Preservation of Natural Conditions. Victor Shelford, the first president of the ESA and a strong supporter of the work of the committee, transferred the committee's work to a home outside the association. The nonprofessional organization that Shelford founded to house these advocacy activities later morphed into The Nature Conservancy.

The silence imposed on ecologists ended in the revolutionary sixties when respected professionals began to voice warnings about thinning connections in the biological matrix that sustained human life. Rachel Carson's *Silent Spring* (1962) is usually cited as the watershed between unengaged and engaged ecology. A few ecologists muttered about the precipitate marriage of politics and ecology, but the media embraced the new move. The period from the 1970s to the present has seen the steady expansion of a more mature and confident science into once-forbidden subjects. Today the ESA, with its ten thousand members, is twice the size of the BSA. Ecology has transformed itself into an academic study that now frames the more restricted research of biologists, zoologists, botanists, and biochemists. The child of biology—if it ever was that—has become the parent.

∾

Surging interest in ecology over the last fifty years has contributed a number of new words to the English language. *Ecosystem*, coined in the 1930s as a collective term for the physical and biotic components of the environments studied by ecologists, quickly became the flagship concept of modern ecology. The textbook from which modern ecologists learned their craft, Eugene Odum's 1953 *Fundamentals of Ecology*, gave early prominence to the term. By the time the text's third edition was published in 1970, *ecosystem* had become the longest entry in the index. A 1986 survey of members of the British Ecological Society ranked the term as the most important concept in ecology, giving it almost twice the prominence of second-tier concepts. The Declaration on Environment and Development adopted at the 1992 Rio Summit used the term in its summary of the environmental responsibilities of member states. By the turn of the millennium, more than a hundred US federal statutes employed *ecosystem* somewhere in their texts.

An ecosystem, says one modern dictionary, is "a community of organisms and its environment functioning as an ecological unit." The idea that an ecosystem is the basic unit of ecology, in the same way that the atom is the basic unit of chemistry and the cell is the basic unit of biology, is widespread. Ask someone today what an ecologist does and you are likely to hear that he or she "studies ecosystems." Credentialed biologists, botanists, and ecologists, however, are less certain than the public about the ecosystems that are supposed to be the focus of their work. A number of professionals have argued that ecosystems are nothing more than academic inventions. The reality of ecosystems, they say, has more to do with the agenda of the person using the word than with the natural systems being studied. Skeptical voices were heard in the early days of ecology, mounted to a crescendo in the 1960s and 1970s, and continue to be heard today.

The foundation for the modern debate over the nature of ecosystems was laid in the last decade of the nineteenth century. At that time, the focus of ecological research was on plant communities, groups of inter-relating plants occupying distinct habitats. Ecological ideas about plant communities in this period tended to circulate around two widely spaced intellectual poles. In much of Europe, especially in Germany, academic perspectives were influenced by the traditions of *idealism*. Idealists also held several important chairs of philosophy in North American universities. Another perspective that had grown up alongside idealism, *positivism*, was more common in France and England. It also had a strong presence in North America, where positivist ideas were taken up and promoted by the American pragmatists. The differences between these two schools of thought, idealism and positivism, can be subtle and complex. Only one difference concerns us here, however. Idealists generally give more weight to collections; positivists tend to see collections in terms of the components that make up the collections.

In Europe, the study of plant communities at the end of the nineteenth century was carried out by the ecologists that eventually formed the various schools of European phytosociology. The European approach quickly spread around the globe—in the previous chapter, we looked at how this movement was transplanted to Canada. The prevailing climate of idealism on the European continent licensed the phytosociologists, wherever they went, to study large natural conglomerates.* Plant community researchers trained in these schools did not have to defend their assumption that these conglomerates were real. In areas of the world that were less attached to the traditions of idealism, however, researchers began to question these assumptions. Those who were influenced by positivism felt uncomfortable with the broad collective terms employed by phytosociologists.

The tensions between idealism and positivism defined the career of Frederic Clements, a mentor and friend of ESA president Victor Shelford. Clements was the leading North American player in the new science of ecology during the first decades of the twentieth century. He was influ-

---

*A number of other sciences were attracted by the organism metaphor in the late nineteenth century. Arsène Darmesteter, writing in the 1880s, began his lectures on linguistics with the line, "It is a commonplace truth today that languages are living organisms whose life . . . is no less real than, and can be compared to, that of organisms in the plant and animal kingdoms."

enced, as the European phytosociologists were, by the assumptions of idealism. Clements's writings highlighted the importance of larger units of vegetation and downplayed the status of the plants that made up the units. His colleagues and successors took issue with his unswerving faith in these larger groupings. By the end of his career, Clements's research seemed tainted by its attachment to a philosophical framework that his fellow ecologists no longer accepted.

The young Clements studied biology at the University of Nebraska. He enrolled in the new Department of Botany that Charles Bessey founded in 1884. Bessey, before he came to Nebraska, had already gained a national reputation for his high school botany textbooks. Dur-

Frederic and Edith Clements spent summers in their Alpine Laboratory near Pikes Peak. Pictured with Frederic and Edith (topmost pair of the sitting group) are employees and disciples. Taken about the time of World War I, from Box 69, Folder 1, Edith S. and Frederic E. Clements Papers, Collection Number 01678, American Heritage Center, University of Wyoming.

ing his thirty years at Nebraska, Bessey would launch a number of his university students into careers in ecology—in the first half of the twentieth century more students would receive postsecondary and graduate degrees in grassland ecology from the University of Nebraska than from all other American institutions combined. Frederic Clements and Roscoe Pound, two of Bessey's earliest students, collaborated for their doctoral theses on the first statewide study of Nebraska plant communities. Roscoe Pound would later return to his earlier interest in law and become famous for his work in American jurisprudence, but in the late 1890s both he and Clements gave their undivided attention to ecological topics. They struggled to find a way to pursue ecological questions in a way that was scientifically respectable. The two of them pored over the German botanical literature that Bessey procured for them, absorbing the underlying perspectives of German idealism.*

After Pound headed to Harvard to study law, Clements stayed on at the University of Nebraska, teaching classes in botany and ecology for Bessey's department. He later transferred to the University of Minnesota to chair its Department of Botany. Two decades into his academic career, Clements took up a post with the Carnegie Institution in Washington, to become, as he said, an "escaped professor." For the next quarter of a century Carnegie provided him with generous funds to hire research assistants and carry out a series of ecological studies in several regions of the United States. Clements investigated the botanical clusters then known as *formations*, ecosystems grouped into inclusive categories of grasslands, forests, marshlands, and so on. In 1939, a few years before his death, Clements coauthored with his friend Shelford a book (*Bio-Ecology*) that extended Clements's work on plants and their formations into larger plant/animal communities.

---

*The Nebraska names in these paragraphs were, for the most part, unfamiliar to those of us who received a high school education in the state. The exception is Charles Bessey, who was renowned for his work in setting up the Nebraska National Forest at Halsey, Nebraska. The forest—perhaps the largest human-planted forest in North America—resides in a region of natural grasslands. The forest is maintained today by large infusions of federal and state money. Workers at the forest plant trees that do not seed themselves and suppress the fires trying to return the forests to grasslands. In 1965, I was part of a huge crew of high school students who streamed from all across central Nebraska to fight a fire in Halsey that claimed a third of Bessey's artificial forest.

Clements wrote in one of his first books that the study of plants "necessarily rests upon the assumption that the unit or climax formation is an organic entity." Though he pioneered an impressive list of research practices and concepts during his fifty-year career, Clements is today remembered for two notions, both of them embedded in this early sentence. The first notion is that ecosystems progress toward a mature state called a *climax*. The second, related, notion is his conviction that ecosystems are organisms. Clements believed that ecosystems expressed, over their life cycles, the same kinds of physiological responses that we associate with living creatures. Like organisms, biotic communities could develop, mature, and die. In later books, Clements would compare the components of such communities to the organs of a body. Just as organs in the body take their meanings from the roles they play in the larger organism, the individual plants in a plant community realize their purpose as parts of a larger whole. This claim, which gives Clements's approach to ecology the name of *organicism*, is so bold that some have argued that it must be a metaphor. Clements, however, did not regard language about species as literal and the words about ecological systems as metaphors. Nurtured in the traditions of idealism, he believed that the communities of plants described in his studies were at least as authentic as the species categories that biology had inherited from natural philosophy. His strongest statement on the topic, written in 1916, asserts that a plant community, like an animal, "is a unified mechanism in which the whole is greater than the sum of its parts" and that this mechanism "constitutes a new kind of organic being with novel properties."

One of the earliest ecologists to raise questions about Clements's organic view of ecosystems was Henry Gleason. Gleason, who launched his career in ecology a decade later than Clements, began his studies inside the framework laid out in Clements's publications. Accumulating doubt, however, soon forced him to abandon some of the assumptions of idealism. What gave rise to a community of plants, Gleason came to believe, was the shared tolerance of the individual species for certain environmental conditions. A plant community, he would later write, was not an organism, but "merely the fortuitous juxtaposition of plants." Clements, he claimed, had missed this fact because he did not understand the difference between an organization and an organism.

Gleason's complaint was a lonely one when he first voiced it in the 1910s. The traditions of positivism were gaining ground in North America during this period, however, and by the second and third decades of the twentieth century the line of thought that Gleason pioneered had picked up a large number of followers. In an early chapter of his 1939 *Bio-Ecology*, Clements introduces a clippings file of quotations to show that scientists from many fields—entomologists, sociologists, evolutionists—were boarding the organicism bandwagon. He mentions no opposing viewpoints when he reaffirms that a plant and animal community is "a complex organism, or superorganism, with characteristic development and structure" and that it possesses "characteristics, powers, and potentialities not belonging to any of its constituents or parts." But the very presence of the clippings file at the head of the book tells us what Clements dared not admit: a significant opposition was gaining force. By the 1950s, a large number, perhaps even a majority, of North American ecologists and botanists had edged into Gleason's camp.

Robert Whittaker took up Gleason's line of reasoning and led an individualistic dissent from the picture of plant communities promoted by the idealist framework of Clements and the European phytosociologists. "Species," Whittaker argues, "do not fit naturally into groupings." Ecosystems, he believed, were arbitrary collections of species whose boundaries were decreed, not by nature, but by the ecologist. Whittaker sought to replace the artificial clustering of species inside ecosystem categories with what he called *gradient analysis*. In gradient analysis, certain environmental factors—elevation, temperature, soil acidity, humidity, and so on—are selected for study, and the plant species in a given region are ranked according to their toleration of the ranges of values, the gradients, assumed by the factors. The result is a series of curves, one for each species, showing the response of the various species to incremental changes in the environmental factors. The curves are then merged. Large overlaps in the areas under the curves correspond to species that are traditionally lumped into communities. A plant community, by this analysis, is a set of species displaying similar responses to the environmental factors that affect plant growth in a region. Calling it a community does not imply that the collection of plant species is more than the sum of the species and their individual responses.

Through the middle decades of the twentieth century, North Americans doing botanical and ecological research inched, slowly and steadily, toward the individualistic ideas of Whittaker and his colleagues. Plant associations became "a temporary gathering of strangers, a clustering of

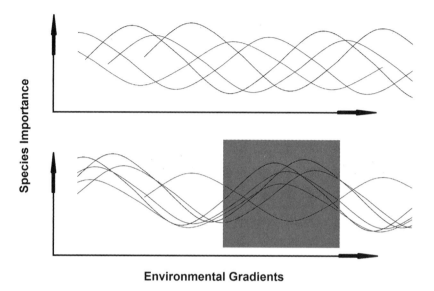

Environmental Gradients

To do gradient analysis, biologists map the way species respond to changes in environmental factors. In the top section, responses seem to vary at random. In the bottom section, a common set of responses (shaded area) indicate an "ecosystem."

species unrelated to one another, here for a brief while today, on their way somewhere else tomorrow." The movement away from organicism stumbled, however, in the 1970s. Ecologists suddenly began to pay more attention to the connections between organisms in the same physical environment. Groups of grazers, they noticed, seem to cooperate in a way that extracted maximum nutrients from savannahs and grasslands. Soil decomposers worked together to recycle the nutrients of dead organisms, employing a division of labor that would not be out of place on an assembly line. Restoration of keystone species in degraded environments, such as the wolves in Yellowstone National Park and the sea otters off the coasts of Alaska and British Columbia, generated cascades of responses at all levels of the restored ecosystems. If studying ecosystems as wholes brought new insights into the workings of natural environments, ecologists asked, should researchers confine themselves to tools honed for the study of an ecosystem divided into its constituent gradients and species? By the time ecology entered its second century in the 1990s, positivism had lost some its grip and a measure of idealism was returning to the scientific study of the environment. We can see the effect of this shift in the introduction to a collection of articles from the 2008 *Encyclopedia of Ecology*. Editor Sven Jørgensen writes about the "emerging properties" of the "interacting and connected biotic and abiotic components" of an ecosystem. Ecosystems, he says, "are whole systems and studies of ecosystems dynamics therefore require holistic views." In a comparison that looks like a sentence from Clements, Jørgensen says that "a living organism is much more than the cells and the organs that make up the organism. Similarly, a forest is more than just the trees—it is a cooperative working unit."

We look back at Frederic Clements with a certain sadness. He brought on himself some of the resentment that later ecologists felt about his role in the establishment of North American ecology. Clements, say those who knew him, was a straitlaced fellow who was not overly tolerant of the failings of his friends. Roscoe Pound, borrowing a joke from Mark Twain, quipped that his associate was a man with "no redeeming vices." On topics that interested him, Clements tended to speak and write ex cathedra. We can still hear the imperial tone in the prose of his books. His research colleagues, struggling to maintain their independence, seldom stayed with him for more than a few years, and when he died no school was left behind to carry on his work. Clashes occasioned by personality and professional practices, however, cannot explain the depth of opposition to Clements's vision of holistic ecosystems. Only ideological conflicts generate disagreements of this magnitude. Clements had the misfortune to announce a vision of integrated ecological communities at a time when North American tolerance for the abstractions of idealism was on the wane.

∽

In recent decades, governments have become major consumers of the ecosystem thinking pioneered by Frederic Clements. They employ derived versions of Clements's concepts to manage the land they own. And

they have a lot to manage. Governments hold a staggering amount of
the globe's land surface in trust, even in countries that encourage private
ownership of land. Here in Canada, the second largest country in the
world, almost 90 percent of the land is crown land. From one-quarter to
three-quarters of the land occupied by the western US states consists of
publically owned tracts.

A few of the world's nations hold land passively, taking ownership of
land that private and commercial parties do not need. Most of the world's
governments assume proactive ownership roles, holding back from sale
and development pieces of land that have outstanding environmental
value. According to the World Conservation Monitoring Centre of the
United Nations, almost 13 percent of the earth's land area has been set
aside "to achieve the long-term conservation of nature."

To select these reserved lands in ways that maximize their environmental value, governments must take into account how ecosystems are
distributed through their territories. But what is an ecosystem? How do
we measure its size, draw its boundaries? The Convention on Biological
Diversity, the UN agency that sets goals and measures progress in land
conservation, ties its goals to what it calls *ecological regions*. It says that
these regions are "habitats with important ecological functions such as
grasslands, wetlands, and others." This approach to defining ecosystems
reminds us in its generality of Frederic Clements's climax-tending formations. Ecologists do not agree on a definition for formations, but we
would not be far off the mark in thinking of formations as the broadest
ecological units into which we could parcel a nation's land. If we took a
map of North America and labeled certain regions as deserts, mountains,
tundra, wetlands, and so on, we would have made a formation-sensitive
division of the continent into its constituent parts.

It is national governments, not state/provincial and local governments, that tend to show the greatest interest in these large-scale formations. In Canada, the first public entity to give serious thought to
formation-sized ecological units was Parks Canada, a century-old agency
charged with the management and expansion of Canada's national parks.
Parks Canada, when it began to reflect in the 1970s on its historic role
in land preservation, noted that the twenty parks it then curated had

not been assembled in a systematic way. The agency sought principles
to guide future acquisitions and published the results as the National
Parks System Plan. The plan divided the country into thirty-nine areas.
Naming the sectioned areas *natural regions*, the agency set a goal of estab-
lishing at least one national park in each of these regions. It continues to
adhere to this goal today: as Parks Canada acquires new parks to add to
the forty or so it already manages, it gives priority to the natural regions
of the country that do not already have a park.

Parks Canada didn't publish a scientific rationale for the borders that
it drew on its map of Canada's natural regions. One commentator has
suggested that the agency employed a blindfold test to mark off the

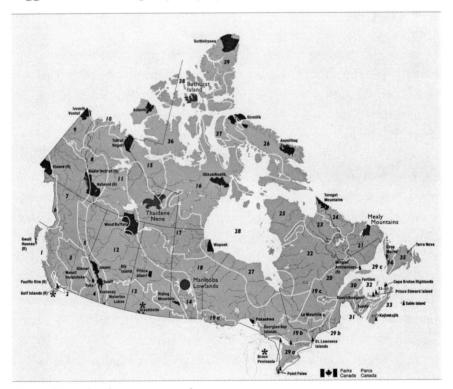

A map of Canada's thirty-nine natural regions.

regions. Imagine a tourist, one who had traveled and camped widely
in Canada, being plopped down in a rural area without knowing how
she had got there. Would she recognize where she was from the landscape, flora, and fauna around her? If so, the locale probably has enough

uniqueness to be designated as one of the country's natural regions. The actual process of defining regions is not quite this informal, but it's hard to avoid the conclusion that tourism plays more of a role than science in determining where to draw the boundaries of the natural regions.

In the last decade, this level of ecosystem granularity—the one we point at with the terms *ecological region, natural region,* or *formation*—has been given more rigorous definition by the Worldwide Fund for Nature (WWF, once known as the World Wildlife Fund). The WWF, the world's largest private organization dedicated to the protection of natural systems, carried out its conservation goals for years without a meaningful map of the ecological regions targeted by its programs. In the late 1990s, WWF charged the personnel in its science program with the task of dividing the world into ecological units. The science program adopted the term *ecoregion* to refer to an area with shared ecological dynamics and a common climate and geography. Currently the WWF recognizes more than eight hundred terrestrial and two hundred marine ecoregions. Canada's land mass, says the WWF, contains about fifty of these ecoregions.

The thirty-nine natural regions of Parks Canada and the fifty ecoregions of the WWF have comparable sizes. Presumably WWF Canada and Parks Canada could, if they needed to, put their heads together and reconcile the numbers. Chances are, though, that the higher number published by the WWF is a better estimation. Not only is it more recent and presumably based on sounder science, it is also in closer agreement with another attempt to carve up Canada into ecological units. In the 1990s, Environment Canada partnered with Agriculture and Agri-Foods Canada to develop a national ecological framework. The two ministries divided Canada into fifteen *ecozones* and a couple of hundred *ecoregions.* While they were busy sorting out these ecological units, NAFTA, the trade agreement between Canada, the United States, and Mexico, came into effect. A side accord of NAFTA set up the Commission on Environment Cooperation (CEC), which started to work on a more comprehensive system of ecological units that would include all three countries. To make its system dovetail with the CEC scheme, Environment Canada added an intermediate level between ecozones and ecoregions that it called *ecoprovinces.* There are, says Environment Canada, just over fifty ecoprovinces in Canada. The US Environmental Protection Association (EPA) also worked with the CEC to organize the land mass of the United States into a series of nested ecological units. It called the granularities Level I, Level II, and so on; Level III in the EPA reckoning corresponds with Environment Canada's ecoprovinces. The EPA put out a map showing more than a hundred Level III units in the United States.

It's easy to get lost in the welter of schemes and agency acronyms, but stepping back brings a few broad facts into focus. First, the decade of the 1990s was, by any account, a golden age for the mapping of ecological regions. Second, national governments find it useful to recognize a relatively coarse level of ecosystem clumping. Third, the word most commonly attached to the units defined by national governments is *ecoregion*. Ecoregions, we note, tend to be one to two hundred thousand square kilometers in size. The upper part of this range would be a fifth of British Columbia, or an area about the size of Missouri. The lower part of the range would be about the size of the state of Maine or the province of New Brunswick.

But are ecoregions good approximations of ecosystems? There are reasons to think they may not be. We would expect ecosystems, if they are real, to announce themselves in ways that scientists could readily measure. Objective tools, however, are rare at the ecoregion level of mapping. What is accepted as evidence for a boundary in one area is not given the same weight in another area. Ecoregion maps, moreover, leave out a lot of lines that good ecologists would like to draw. As a result, almost all of the ecoregion schemes have found it necessary to define, or at least leave the door open to define, smaller units. When the WWF ran a project in Canada during the 1990s called the Endangered Spaces Campaign, it cobbled together some work done in the individual provinces and mapped out about five hundred distinct ecological units, ten times as many as they would later report in their ecoregion research. The Environment Canada maps from the same era define not only the two hundred ecoregion units mentioned above, but also a thousand Canadian *ecodistricts* nested inside the ecoregions. Driven by a similar rationale, the American EPA defined Level IV ecological units within the Level III units. The EPA didn't provide maps for these smaller units, proposing instead that state and local researchers take up the task. A number of these Level IV maps have been produced.

To take a closer look at these finer-grained divisions, we need to turn, as the EPA suggests, to lower levels of government. Consider the way that the provincial government of British Columbia handles the issue of ecological units. The provincial counterpart of Parks Canada is BC Parks. Inside the province, BC Parks has a much bigger task than Parks Canada. The parklands in the hundreds of provincial parks, parks that currently encompass a tenth of the land area of British Columbia, are twenty times larger than the acreage contained in the seven national parks that are sited in the province. The provincial agency, like its federal counterpart, attempts to spread its acquisition and management efforts over the largest number of distinct ecological units. BC Parks lists as its first guiding principle "conserving and managing representative examples of British Columbia's ecosystems" and as its second principle "maintaining essential ecological processes . . . through the conservation and management of complete and functioning ecosystems." The broad federal approach, recognizing only ten or so ecoregions in the province, underrepresents the rich variety of ecosystems in the provincial parklands. Nature is not carved at its joints by federal knives.

But why should we stop at the provincial/state level in our search for meaningful ecosystem boundaries? One could argue that ecosystem maps are like fractal designs—the closer one looks, the more detail one sees. Under some ways of looking at the issue, mud puddles, even water droplets, can be ecosystems. But in this case logic runs roughshod over intuition. Most people regard ecosystems as larger entities. We can see this intuition at work when we descend to the next level of park management in British Columbia. The political map of the province divides it into about sixty regional districts. These would correspond to the county level of government in the United States and the rest of Canada. The regional district where I live, the one that includes the greater Victoria area, owns a significant amount of parkland—at present it manages more than eleven thousand hectares of land contained in some thirty distinct parks. The park management goals published by my local regional district use phrases such as "maintaining ecosystem services," but they don't say much about distributing conservation efforts over as many

ecosystems as possible. The feeling conveyed by these regional documents is that relatively few ecosystems are represented in the lands
managed by a given district. In the perspective both of the public and
of science, the definition of North American ecosystems belongs, most
naturally, not to the district/county level, but to the governments of the
provinces/states/estados of Canada, the United States, and Mexico.

Let's return, then, to how this middle level of government draws its
lines around ecological units. In British Columbia, the Ministry of the
Environment began to construct a classification system in the 1980s. In
the early 1990s, the system was revised and extended to accommodate
the many streams of ecoregion thinking that were pouring in from the
national government and from the international CEC. Ministry researchers struggled to adapt patterns that had been created for the prairies and
the Ontario-Quebec heartlands. The broad regions defined in the rest
of Canada, scientists finally decided, were too inclusive for the variable
forest landscapes of Canada's western mountains and coasts. A more
detailed map would be needed. Eventually the ecoprovinces and ecodistricts popular in the other provinces were bypassed and the Ministry of
the Environment settled, in the late 1990s, on a system that had a more
intense clumping of ecoregions—the province was judged to have about
forty of these—subdivided into smaller habitats called *ecosections*. The
new system became the basis for decisions made in the Wildlife Branch
of the ministry and, to a lesser extent, for choices made by BC Parks.

The ecoregion/ecosection classification of the Ministry of the Environment is not the only show in town, however. The bulk of British
Columbia's public lands—three-quarters of it—is crown forest. These
lands are managed by another ministry, Forests and Range.* For the last
three decades the Research Branch of this ministry has kept a team of
forest ecologists busy with what it has dubbed the *Biogeoclimatic Ecosystem
Classification*, the BEC.

When I moved to British Columbia, I started to hear local naturalists
using phrases based on the BEC. They would talk about a certain region
of a forest as a "cedar/sword fern variant of the Coastal Douglas-fir zone."

---

*Now called the Ministry of Forests, Lands, and Natural Resource Operations. The
ministry changes its name with disconcerting regularity.

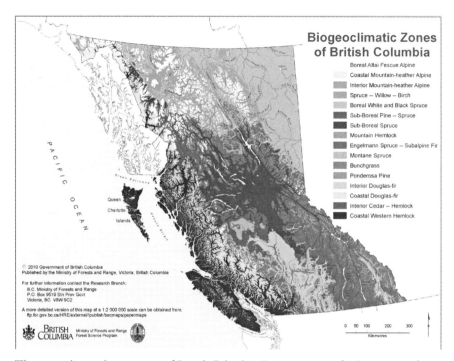

The sixteen biogeoclimatic zones of British Columbia. Image courtesy of BC Ministry of Forests and Range.

The terminology surprised me. I was not accustomed to naming habitats by such specific vegetative patterns. The BEC, I would eventually learn, had mined phytosociological sources to come up with a way to recognize ecosystems from surveys of plants. A quick comparison of the BEC map of British Columbia and a map based on the Ministry of Environment's ecoregions shows the difference in orientation. A BEC map of the sixteen biogeoclimatic zones in the province has details at the boundaries between zones that maps of ecoregions do not display. One zone reaches into another with deep peninsulas and stranded islands. Only on-site surveys could provide such a welter of wandering lines.

As we drill down into the research behind the BEC and its maps, we discover that the basic ecological unit is not the zone shown on the map but a subdivision of the zone called a *subzone*. With most of British Columbia surveyed, about 150 of these BEC subzones have been defined. The ecoregion approach of the Ministry of the Environment, we note, also divides the province into about the same number of ecosections. Because they use different methods to draw their lines, the boundaries recognized by the two systems do not always coincide. What is interest-ing about the convergence in numbers, though, is that those who work with natural systems find it useful, no matter what system they employ, to divide the forested lands of the Pacific Northwest into areas that aver-age about seventy thousand square kilometers. In their drive to maintain a formal scientific approach, they give them jawbreaking names such as *biogeoclimatic subzones, ecosections,* and *ecodistricts.* I prefer to think that we approach, in these finer divisions, the fabled *ecosystems,* the traditional basic units of ecology.

∾

That's what ecosystems/biogeoclimatic zones look like from the outside. But what do they look like from the inside? I've got one of the BEC experts in front of me. Andy has been part of the Ministry of Forests and Range mapping team from the beginning.

"How would you define a biogeoclimatic zone?" I ask.

"One way to describe a biogeoclimatic zone is to say that it is an area of broadly homogeneous climate as it is reflected in the vegetation."

"Climate? You mean weather?"

"Climate is weather over a long period. But long-term weather pat-terns determine more than just how hot or cold, wet or dry a region is. Climate forms soils, for example. In this area of Vancouver Island, which is in the Coastal Douglas-fir biogeo-climatic zone, our soils are not the same as those found in the Coastal Western Hemlock zone on the west side of the island. There they get much more rain and the rain leaches minerals from the upper layers of the soil. Distinct soil horizons develop

Andy MacKinnon.

and very little mixing occurs. Here, however, there is less leaching and our soils support the European earthworms that blend the soil layers even further.

"Climate also affects settlement patterns. When you read the writings of British Columbia's first explorers and administrators, you notice that they differentiate the weather patterns on the southeastern end of Vancouver Island from weather in the rest of the province. When James Douglas saw this part of the island, he wrote that 'the place appears a perfect Eden in the midst of the dreary wilderness of the Northwest coast.' The mild climate that Douglas noted attracted settlers. Because people settled here first, development happened here first. We have had more time, as a result, to overrun native ecosystems. In this area of the province we have the highest percentage of urban and agricultural land and the lowest percentage of native forest.

"The absence or presence of fire is also a result of climate. Over most of North America fire is an important agent of disturbance. It determines wildlife habitat and forest succession. On the wet west side of Vancouver Island we don't get many fires, so the wilderness landscape is predominantly old-growth forest. In the rest of Canada's forests, fire is a factor, and the forested landscape displays a mixture of stand ages."

"So you draw the boundaries of the biogeoclimatic zones by measuring climate?" I ask.

"If we had enough weather stations, and data over a long enough period of time, we could use climate data directly. We don't have weather data at this density, however, so we have to use vegetation patterns to infer climate. We have collected data on vegetation coverage from about fifty thousand plots over the last thirty to forty years. It is the use of this data that makes our classification of ecosystems fundamentally different from most other attempts to define ecological regions. The biogeoclimatic classification system derives, in a sense, from the methods of European botany that came into British Columbia with V. J. Krajina and his students. We use their methodologies and we have the same strong view of ecosystems that the Europeans have."

"So how do you map a biogeoclimatic zone?"

"We're doing some maps right now for the island of Haida Gwaii. We have a number of vegetation plot measurements for the island—perhaps twelve hundred of them. These have come from different groups who have studied Haida Gwaii vegetation. When we pull all this data together, we notice that the tree cover of the west side of the island tends to be sitka spruce and western hemlock with an understory dominated by deer fern. So we group these plots and apply ordination techniques that allow us to analyze similarities and differences between the individual plots. We generalize the data from the plots and come up with an average plot, one that has a plant coverage that approaches the theoretical mean. This allows us to describe a zonal association, a community of plants that occurs on a site that is not at the extremes of wetness, dryness, etc., for the area we are studying. We then look at the plots and see where this association of plants occurs on sites that fall within a certain range of the average for moisture, temperature, and elevation. The matching plots are designated as zonal plots. We draw a line around these zonal plots and that region becomes a biogeoclimatic subzone."

"How does this differ from other systems that are used to map ecological regions?"

"The biogeoclimatic zone is a British Columbia innovation. But you can find similarities with the rest of Canada and the United States. We have plant associations, US researchers have their habitat types, but they are essentially the same thing. Outside of British Columbia, however, these plant communities are not usually represented as occurring within climate-defined geographical units. Because the climate correlations are not made, the other systems don't always recognize what we think are important differences."

I leaf through a folder of printouts I brought along and show Andy a description of the ecoregions and ecosections of British Columbia. "The provincial government has two systems of ecosystem classification, doesn't it? There is the one you work on, but there is also the one used by the Ministry of Environment."

"These are compatible classification systems. The one maintained by the Wildlife Branch of the Ministry of Environment puts more emphasis on land forms and the territories of the large ungulates that they monitor. If an area is mountainous, we would tend to recognize different zones in the different plant communities—alpine, montane, and so on. They would tend to put the whole mountain into a single region because the animals they want to protect move through the various plant communities."

"What about the future? Is support for biogeoclimatic mapping strong?"

"If you had asked me that last year, I would have said yes. Now I'm not so sure. The ministry I work for has seen some serious layoffs. A lot of the layoffs in the interior of British Columbia were concentrated in the ecology programs of the Research Branch. A few years ago, those of us who had spent our working lives developing and maintaining the ecological classifications used in forestry management went to the ministry and asked permission to hire new researchers. We were all getting close to retirement and we wondered who would carry on the work. Maintaining continuity seemed like a responsible strategy. As a result of this request, seven new researchers were hired to help the four of us that were covering the various regions of British Columbia. In the last nine months, two of the older people have retired. When they retired, their positions disappeared. At the same time, four of the younger researchers were let go. We are now wondering how firm the provincial government's commitment to ecosystem classification really is."

∾

Andy tells me about the cuts to the BEC research program with a Scottish dispassion. I know, though, that he feels strongly about what is happening at his workplace. And well he should. It would be ironic if the decline of forestry in British Columbia should remove one resource threat to the environment—the overextraction of timber—while depriving the province of a basic tool—an ongoing province-wide map of biogeoclimatic zones—that it needs to manage its remaining resources.

Over the last century, a new science, as we noted earlier, has shaped itself around the term *ecology*. An important goal of the science of ecology has been the description of autonomous, integrated environmental units. If the goal is achieved, the globe will one day be laced with a network of meandering lines marking out several thousand unique ecosystems. A global ecosystem map, a genome of the environment, would have a wealth of applications. The collated observations of climate, soils, and vegetation in British Columbia's BEC, originally designed to manage forests, have proved useful in provincial plant science, restoration, and land use planning.

The journey of ecology to science status has not, however, been an easy one. Conflict has dogged its every step. A history-of-ideas review of the conflicts finds traces of idealism on one side of the conflict, positivism on the other. The two frameworks, fueled by ambiguities in the term *ecosystem*, stood at maximum opposition in the 1980s. In recent decades, a boundary layer between these frameworks has begun to open up. In this boundary layer, the abstractions of the larger philosophies are replaced by more practical mandates. The day-to-day and year-to-year needs of those who manage public land have given us a clearer idea of what an ecosystem is. While these rough-and-ready ecosystems may not be Clements's climax-trending organisms, neither are they random collections of species with similar tolerances to local conditions. The sooner we can finish our world ecosystem map, the sooner we can extend what we have learned in our public management boundary layer into the swirl of broad ideas that originally created the boundary.

When we get to the place where we can turn our experiences with on-the-ground ecosystems into a tool that will help us grasp the role of species in their larger environmental settings, we may find that one group of species scientists, the ones who study lichens, have got there first. A Pacific Northwest lichenologist has become one of the early explorers of this new species-ecosystem boundary layer. For years I've been hearing him referenced and quoted. He's become a bit of a recluse, however, so our paths have yet to cross. My next trip will take me to his hermitage.

∾

Nameless Lichens

A silver-haired man steps from the shadows of the hallway and reaches down to shake my hand. I'm taller than the average North American but Trevor Goward has me by at least a head. He looks, on first impression, a lot like the Swedish actor Max von Sydow.

To get to Trevor's house was a day's trip. I left my home before dawn and the sun was already setting when I turned the car toward the narrow, twenty-kilometer corridor of private land that reaches into British Columbia's Wells Gray Park. At the turn-in to Edgewood, Trevor's property, my view of the mountain terrain was no

Trevor Goward with Orca. Photograph by Virginia Skilton.

wider than the car's high beams. The house numbers, set back from the road, were hard to see. I missed the entrance on the first pass.

Trevor moved to Edgewood in order to anchor a peripatetic life. He was born in Vancouver ("up to that date," he says, "the longest baby born in the city") and started his education there. Urban life didn't suit the young boy. Several times he fled from the city on his bicycle, pedaling across Second Narrows Bridge and into the North Shore Mountains, where he would wander the woods until darkness frightened him home. When Trevor was nine, his family moved to a more rural setting, a small community outside of Kamloops in central British Columbia. There Trevor began to teach himself the local birds and plants, inventing names for them when books and people couldn't help him.

Trevor's legs were stretching and soon even the hills around Kamloops felt too compact, too crowded with people and their histories. He yearned for wilder places where he could walk and walk and not meet anyone. Above all he wanted to be in a place that would not end up like his grandparent's five acres above Burnaby Lake. Trevor had watched as developers subdivided his refuge into an asphalt network of rectilinear streets and alleyways.

What Trevor didn't know in high school was that the wilderness he longed for was not in some distant northern terrain. It was much nearer, on a nature reserve only 150 kilometers north of his Kamloops home. Trevor first entered Wells Gray Provincial Park on a spring school trip. The trip did not come off as planned—the class arrived to find the park road clogged with two feet of snow. The snowbound landscape made a strong impression on the young man, however, and in 1971 Trevor, then a student at Simon Fraser University, applied for summer work at Wells Gray. He started out working on an Opportunities for Youth road crew. Later that summer a park superintendent hired him for a trail unit on Battle Mountain. Trevor tried to learn the names of the mountain's alpine wildflowers during breaks from the work. Over the next two years he mastered enough plant taxonomy to lay claim to a position as park naturalist. He was employed as a Wells Gray naturalist on and off for thirteen years. In addition to the park's flowering plants, Trevor got to know the birds, mammals, insects, mushrooms, vegetation zonation, volcanic geology, and lichens. He teamed up with a colleague to condense what he was learning into the book *Nature Wells Gray*, a natural history of the park.

It was the last of his natural history subjects, the lichens of Wells Gray, that would bind Trevor to the park. In the mid-1970s, during the final year of his undergraduate studies at New Brunswick's Mount Allison University, he had sat in on biology courses taught by Hinrich Harries. Harries helped Trevor and a handful of his classmates carry out an intense study of local East Coast lichens. Once back in Wells Gray, Trevor began to collect the lichens of the West Coast. He made contact in the course of his lichen studies with two of the world's leading lichenologists, Ernie Brodo at the Canadian Museum of Nature and Teuvo Ahti at the University of Helsinki. The bryologist Wilf Schofield also encouraged Trevor's interest in lichens. Trevor would later acknowledge his mentors by naming after them two lichen genera, *Ahtiana* and *Brodoa*, and a species, *Hypogymnia wilfiana*.

Trevor's expanding interest in lichens took him to many of the natural regions of the Pacific Northwest in the late 1970s and early 1980s. It also brought him back, in the end, to Wells Gray. Half of British Columbia's two thousand species of lichens, Trevor discovered on his trips through the park, had found homes inside the reserve. He acquired title to a tract of land next to the park in 1984 and built a house on it. Edgewood, surrounded on three sides by Wells Gray Park, became the wilderness home he had dreamed about.

By the late 1990s, the Edgewood-based Trevor had authored and coauthored two sets of illustrated keys to provincial lichens. In chasing down the province's lichens, he turned up several dozen species that had not been described before. The radiance of his passion for lichens, however, hid creeping shadows from him. Trevor did not know it, but he was heading for an emotional and intellectual crisis.

∾

Trevor stood, in the 1990s, at the edge of a conceptual divide that had opened up two hundred years earlier. The divide separates two ways of studying biological systems. On one side stands a succession of scientists who look at the natural world as a playground for species. On the other side are biologists who see the world as an assemblage of ecosystems.

In the last chapter we tracked the widening of this divide over the last century, during the period when ecology was becoming a science. When, though, did the divide first open up? A plausible starting point might be 1808, the year that Alexander von Humboldt moved from Berlin to Paris and began to publish the results of his South American tour.

Humboldt was born into a wealthy Berlin family with close connections to the army and royalty. He and his brother Wilhelm, who would become famous as a statesman and linguist, were caught up in the Romantic movement that swept through Europe in the last decades of the eighteenth century. Alexander displayed an early talent for natural history, but his family pushed him toward finance and politics, grooming him for a career in the Prussian royal service. Before he reached the age of twenty, however, both his parents had died, and Humboldt found himself free to turn his attention and newly acquired fortune to the sciences. After a period of education and some minor European excursions, Humboldt fixed on Central and South America as the place where he could advance his career.

Spanish America at the end of the eighteenth century was a biologi-

cal black hole. Three centuries of European conquest and settlement had left little time for a systematic study of the continent's flora and fauna. Humboldt finagled an authorization from the royal house of Spain to study the plants and animals in their American colonies. He set sail in June 1799 on a self-financed tour, taking along an array of state-of-the-art scientific instruments. He ascended Ecuador's Chimborazo, the Mount Everest of the day, to a height of nearly

Alexander von Humboldt, self-portrait in 1814.

twenty thousand feet—a mountaineering record that would stand for several decades. On his way back to Europe, Humboldt stopped off in the United States and was feted by the intellectual elite who ran the new country. European newspapers, collating the sporadic reports drifting back from Humboldt and others, tracked his five-year tour through Central and South America. By the time he returned to his native Berlin, the botanical explorer had become a media superstar.

When Humboldt began to contemplate the publication of his scientific studies of Central and South America, a task that would eventually run to thirty volumes and consume the remainder of his inheritance, he decided that Paris, and only Paris, had the intellectual and literary resources that the job required. Humboldt left Berlin in 1808 and began his long residence in the City of Light. During his twenty years in France, he became a central node in the interconnecting lines of nineteenth century science. Humboldt met and corresponded with every thinker of note and nurtured many of the young researchers who would construct the scientific establishment that matured later in the century. In her book *Passage to Cosmos*, Laura Dassow Walls points out that Adolphe Quetelet "built on Humboldt's . . . work to found the science of statistics; Justus Liebig founded organic chemistry and claimed he owed his career to Humboldt; Charles Lyell worked with Humboldt in 1823 and likely derived from him the concept of dating rocks from fossils; Louis Agassiz was about to give up on his scientific career when Humboldt took him in." Darwin packed along on *The Beagle* a copy of *Personal Narrative*, Humboldt's popular summary of his American journeys, employing the text both as an inspirational manual and a travel guide. Darwin later lauded Humboldt as "the greatest scientific traveler who ever lived" and said that Humboldt inspired him to undertake his own voyage of biological discovery.

From his South and Central American travels, Humboldt sent back specimens of some six thousand species of plants and animals, half of them new to science. The biology that he had learned as a young man, with its emphasis on the classification of species, would have ranked Humboldt's impressive collection at the top of the list of accomplishments from his five-year tour of the Americas. For Humboldt, though, naming and describing species was a beginning, not an end. His own work concentrated on what he called *plant geography*, the way that vegetation patterns responded to changes in altitude, winds, temperature, climate, and sun. He preferred, he explained in *Personal Narrative*, "the connection of facts . . . to the knowledge of insulated facts. . . . The discovery of an unknown genus seemed to me far less interesting than an observation on the geographical relations of the vegetable world."

A new perspective on biological systems emerged from Humboldt's Romantic attachment to the underlying unity of the natural world. Anyone who uses the word *ecosystem* in a way that implies it is more than just a loose assemblage of organisms writes a check on an account that Humboldt opened more than two hundred years ago. We can see traces of Humboldt's radical ideas in the phytosociological schools that came to dominate European botany. His ideas surface in the ecosystem classifications inspired by Frederic Clements. They also underlie the politics-charged ecology of the counterculture generation.

❧

Just as Carl Linnaeus secured a reputation as the modern founder of species and systematics, Alexander von Humboldt positioned himself at the head of a tradition of ecosystem thinking. These two perspectives, as we have seen, still contend for attention in modern biology. Many of the current debates, when pushed to the level of assumptions, force us to choose between species and ecosystems. Do we side with Humboldt or Linnaeus, European phytosociology or American economic ecology, Frederic Clements or Robert Whittaker? Whenever we putter about our home in the natural world and try to think about how it works, we are distracted by the basement clatter of concepts knocking against each other.

The polarized species and ecosystem approaches do more than wage war. They also form an active boundary layer between them. In recent decades science has turned its attention to a number of natural processes that make their homes in this borderland between species and ecosystems. These processes, because they take on the characteristics we attribute to individual species, can be described with species language. They are also, however, composed of tightly knit communities and can be depicted by words that we normally apply to ecosystems.

We looked at one of these hybrid spaces in an earlier chapter. Mycorrhizal fungi form intimate partnerships with their host species, partnerships that seem to be plant-and-fungus rather than plants with fungal symbionts or fungi with plant symbionts. In recent decades, other biological processes have also taken up residence in the species-ecosystem borderlands. Let's take a quick look at three of these recent immigrants.

The basic unit of the earth's living systems, the cell, has changed over the last billion years. When all life was single-celled, or at best a conglomeration of cells stuck together into a living mat, cells were small and simple, with almost no internal structures. The cell walls surrounded an undifferentiated protoplasmic soup. Biochemical activities inside the walls occurred whenever and wherever. Modern representatives of this earliest stage of cellular life would be the bacteria. Eventually multicellular organisms appeared with larger, internally differentiated cells. The line of evolution that leads from simple bacteria-like cells to the complex cells of multicellular organisms was at one time thought to be straight and gradual, with simple cells acquiring internal structures—nuclei, mitochondria, plastids, and so on—through the microsteps of evolutionary trial and error.

At the beginning of the twentieth century, a few scientists began to question this standard story of cell evolution. They suggested that larger cells may have taken over smaller cells holus-bolus and transformed them into internal organelles. This was a minority view until the discovery in the 1960s that some of these organelles had their own DNA. The biologist Lynn Margulis, wife of astronomer Carl Sagan, championed the minority cause, renaming the process of organelle acquisition *endosymbiosis*. Her daring 1967 paper on endosymbiosis was rejected by over a dozen journals before it was printed. Today it is Margulis's theory that is considered to be the standard account of cellular evolution.

Although the plastids and mitochondria inside cells have their own DNA, they don't have enough of it to survive on their own. Part of the genetic code used by these cell structures, it appears, has been absorbed into the intranuclear code of the cells that contain them. This sort of DNA migration has led some theorists to propose that even cell structures without their own DNA may have had their origin as absorbed single-celled organisms. Margulis, for example, now suggests that the hairlike strands that some cells use to move liquid past their outer walls may be the acquired descendants of coil-shaped bacteria. Some biologists have proposed that the cell nucleus itself may have been the first conquest of the earliest and most undifferentiated cells, perhaps the much-altered remnant of a virus or other primitive organism.

Whether or not the more speculative additions to endosymbiosis make it into the standard story, it is already clear that a modern, complex cell bears a strong resemblance to an ecological community. A cell is, in essence, a group of smaller organisms that have learned to operate as a unit. When we analyze the behavior of the cells in a multicellular organism, we usually think about the reaction of the cell as a whole. Sometimes, though, we need to think about the effect of outside forces on the individual organelles and the distinct responses made by these cell components. Certain diseases, for example, are best analyzed as breakdowns in the community relationships inside cells.

The vocabulary of ecology has also made inroads into the organisms constructed from endosymbiotic cells. Most multicellular organisms, we are starting to realize, are actually communities of interdependent organisms. We once believed that being infected by a strain of bacteria was a step away from full health. Bacteria inside the skin barrier were *bad*. There were hints about *good* bacteria inside of us, but our ability to peer into the communities of microorganisms living in and on macroorganisms was limited. It was relatively easy to spot an organism that shouldn't be there—the virus that causes smallpox, for example, or the bacterium associated with tuberculosis. Benign microorganisms, however, remained hidden from us, concealed behind a curtain of impotent laboratory procedures. Most of these bacteria, yeasts, and viruses could not be persuaded to grow in petri dishes, and microscopes, even high-resolution microscopes, often could not distinguish one microorganism from another. The curtain on the larger cast of cooperating microorganisms only began to rise when DNA sequencing became cheap.

What the new sequencers showed us about our microbial partners would eventually rewrite textbooks. In the revised story, a human being is actually a partnership of organisms. We have in our bodies some hundred trillion human cells, each bearing our unique genetic signature. The gut of a healthy, unmedicated person contains, however, a hundred trillion smaller cells that do not have our DNA. When we add to the gut bacteria all of the microorganisms in our mouths, nose, skin, lungs, and reproductive organs, we discover that our bodies contain about ten microorganisms for every human cell and that these smaller organisms account for perhaps 10 percent of our body weight and up to 50 percent of the body's metabolic output. The part of our bodies that is uniquely *us*, our genes, is mostly not us: the combined genes in this internal microbiome outnumber human genes a hundred to one.*

Some of these small organisms are just along for the ride, but many of them, it is becoming clear, are coevolved partners that we lose at our peril. The Human Microbiome Project was launched in 2007 to find out more about these interspecies connections. The $100-million-plus study is a conceptual and experimental extension of the Human Genome Project that resulted in the decoding of the human genetic package. Researchers with the Human Microbiome Project hope to define several standard human-and-microbe genomes and to fully sequence the genetic package of hundreds of the more common microbial partners. Specific studies done under the umbrella of the project are investigating the connections between our microbiota and our health, focusing in particular on abdominal pain and ulcers, fevers in young children, and acne and psoriasis. But the medical implications of a closer look at the human microbiota may be matched by the study's conceptual implications. One of the project founders, Jeffrey I. Gordon, argues that our traditional self-concepts should be scrapped. We should view ourselves, not as a static, unitary organism, but as a dynamic composite of microbial and human cells. Our genetic landscape should be considered, he says, "a summation of the genes embedded in our own human genome and in the

---

*Even calling our genes *ours* is an overstatement. We share an astounding number of them with our animal relatives. In addition, nearly a tenth of the base pairs in human DNA may be the remnants of old virus genes.

collective genomes of our body habitat-associated microbial communities." To address the community features of the microbiota, the Human
Microbiome Project invokes ecological perspectives: "Questions about
the human microbiome are new only in terms of the system to which
they apply. Similar questions have inspired and confounded ecologists
working on macroscale ecosystems for decades."

It isn't just mammals that are communities of mutualistic organisms.
The study of these communities has also become a new front for biological research on the lower animals. At a bacteriology lab in Wisconsin,
researchers have uncovered a surprising sequence of ant mutualisms that
nestle inside of each other like matryoshka dolls. Leaf-cutter ants were
first studied as individual organisms in the first half of the nineteenth
century. By the end of the nineteenth century, researchers had became
aware that the ants did not actually eat the leaves that they harvested—
they brought them back to their tunnels to serve as a substrate for a
symbiotic fungus that became their food. The story remained stalled at
this two-organism stage until the 1990s, when another nest fungus, one
that attacked and destroyed the fungal symbiont eaten by the ants, was
discovered. What kept the attacking fungus at bay was an antifungal
microbe that grew as a waxy bloom on the outer skeleton of leaf-cutter
ants. The discovery of this insect-fungus connection, say the researchers, is just one front of an "emerging frontier" of insect symbioses.

Besides being walking microbiomes, and besides being composed of
highly evolved, community-like cells, ants inhabit the species-ecosystem
borderlands in a third way. E. O. Wilson, a biologist-philosopher who has
spent much of his professional life studying ants, adopted *superorganism*, a
term originally proposed in the 1920s by W. M. Wheeler, to describe the
curious status of colony-forming social animals. Many animals, including humans, cooperate as species groups, but mutuality usually occurs
against a larger backdrop of competition between individuals. Colony
animals are different. "By itself," observe Wilson and his research partner
Bert Hölldobler, "one ant is . . . a vast disappointment. It is really no ant
at all. What counts is the entire colony, which is the equivalent of an entire nonsocial organism." Colonies, they say, are "operational units" with
"emergent traits" that we cannot discover by summing the behaviors of

individual ants. A superorganism "exists at a level of biological organization between the organisms that form its unit and the ecosystems, such as a forest patch, of which it is a unit."

Colony superorganisms are one of the evolutionary success stories of the last fifty million years. At this point we have put names to about two million different species of living organisms. About half of the known species are insects. Relatively few of these insect species, about one out of every fifty, are social insects, but they occur in such large numbers—hives and colonies with millions of members are not uncommon—that they make up the bulk of the animal biomass in some ecosystems.

As these teeming communities of insects take on roles once reserved in our conceptual categories for individuals of a species, we again find ourselves dealing with units that can be described both with species language and with the concepts and vocabulary of ecology. What we know in ecology about food webs, ecological niches, divisions of labor, and population dynamics becomes germane to a description of an ant colony whose members behave in other respects like individuals of a species. Even the species-centric language of evolution is stressed by these superorganisms. According to the prevailing Darwinian synthesis, natural selection acts on, and expresses its outcome in, the genes carried by individuals. Wilson and other biologists have begun to wonder, though, whether the target of natural selection, the unit on which it operates, has to be the same as the unit that is changed by evolution. In the social insects, selection pressures may result in individuals that belong to a new species, but the pressure that leads to these new individuals seems to be applied at a community level. "The colony is the unit that we must examine," says Wilson, "in order to understand the biology and evolution of both the colony and the ant that is part of it."

∽

Mycorrhizal links, cellular endosymbiosis, microbial communities, social superorganisms—the borderland between species and ecosystems is filling up. We have to wonder who will be the next immigrant to move into the species-ecosystem boundary layer. Before we look too hard for new residents, though, we should acknowledge the oldest member of the neighborhood. The first-described resident of the species-ecosystem boundary layer may have been the compound organisms we call lichens.

Before their compound nature was recognized, researchers assumed that lichens were unary organisms, that they took the same approach to individuality that we impose on most organisms. It's easy to see why lichenologists believed this. The lichens they saw in the field grew, thrived, and died just as other organisms did. They appeared to reproduce true to species type. The organism's individual partners, if they existed, were never seen without their companions.

Microscopes gave us the first clue that lichens were not what they appeared to be. The instruments employed in the first half of the nineteenth century were not able to resolve the lichen subunits. Microscope technology was improving, though, and in the 1860s the Swiss biologist Simon Schwendener, author of a classroom text on botanical microscopy, announced that the green bits that researchers were finding in lichens were actually independent organisms.

Lichenologists of the day were not convinced by Schwendener's claims. Through the rest of the nineteenth century, debate about the "dual hypothesis" continued to rile and roil botanical gatherings. The issue was not decisively settled until just before World War II, when the fungal and algal components of a lichen were separated, cultivated, and recombined under laboratory conditions. The dual hypothesis was difficult for lichen researchers to accept because it ran counter to recently adopted assumptions about biological research. During the last decades of the nineteenth century, scientists were struggling to reconcile the new evolutionary perspective and its view of mutable species with older concepts of static species. Enlisting the science of genetics, they introduced

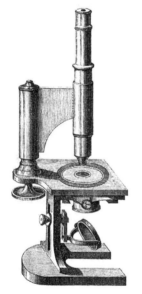

Depiction of microscope from the 1867 Das Mikroskop by Carl Nägeli and Simon Schwendener.

chromosome-coded genotypes, hidden genetic caches, to explain the persistent phenotypes, the appearances and behaviors, of organisms. A unique genotypic package, they posited, gave rise to a corresponding phenotypic package. When the phenotypes of two organisms differed in a significant way, the visible differences pointed to an underlying difference in the invisible genotype. When phenotypes showed less-significant differences, as in the case of varieties and subspecies, they were interpreted as minor variations in what was the same, or essentially the same, underlying genetic code. Through this line of reasoning, the notion of a species became, through gradual steps, a story about genes and genotypes. The abstract idea of a species, which had once pointed to the inscrutable plans of a creator, shifted to the equally abstract idea of a robust and enduring genetic deposit in the data banks of organic information. The new view of lichens suggested by Schwendener's microscopic work was difficult to accept because it did not fit this genetic rethinking of species. There was no room, in the revised understanding, for organisms that had two genotypes with two independent evolutionary histories.

As the evidence for the dual hypothesis began to mount, researchers attempted to banish lichens from the new biological order. Lichenologists, however, were loath to throw away the traditions of lichen classification that were based on single-species assumptions. In the end, a compromise was reached. The species language applied to composite lichens would be attached to the single dominant partner, the fungus or the alga, that did qualify as a species. In the meantime, however, the species assumptions in the biological order that had forced lichenologists to adopt this rule were being challenged. By the end of the twentieth century, novel ways of talking about organisms, ways that emphasized the relationship of organisms to their environmental partners, were becoming more popular. Humboldt's spiritual descendants had made a new science, ecology, out of their ancestor's defection from narrower species perspectives. The new terms and concepts popularized by ecologists seemed to be custom-made for lichen researchers. Lichenologists, however, after decades of compromises with a species perspective, were not sure that they were ready to leave the niche they had worked so hard to carve out.

∽

Trevor Goward began his work on lichens in the framework of a traditional species perspective. In the lichen guide he penned in the 1990s, Trevor coined the definition, "lichens are fungi that have discovered agriculture," a phrase later picked up by the wider scientific community. But at the turn of the twenty-first century Trevor's way of looking at lichens was changing. He and a few other lichenologists were adopting the new conceptual tools being developed by ecologists and applying them to lichen partnerships.

The shift in Trevor's perspective in the mid-1990s had both an emotional and an intellectual dimension. The emotional change was the more abrupt. For most of his adult life, he had been plagued by prolonged bouts of melancholy, a family condition that had affected at least one male family member over several generations. In some cases the affliction had led to suicide. By the time Trevor was in his forties, he was on the verge of becoming the next casualty in the family line. A sustained period of depression, coupled with frequent anxiety attacks, had rendered his life unbearable. "I was alone in those days," he says, "and working day and night to complete the second volume on British Columbia macrolichens. My body was a wreck—I was a human skeleton, about sixty pounds less than I weigh today—and my mind had literally turned on itself. Only the work kept me going. I vowed to see the manuscript through to publication and then, as a 'reward,' as suicides sometimes say, to cash in. At the time—it's hard to make sense of this now—I thought that I must have cancer or some other terminal illness. In the end, I became so weak that I consulted a doctor. He was appalled at my condition. He told me I was suffering from acute depression and that I ought to try a course of medication."

Consenting to take the medication was a huge step for Trevor. He had lived his life without mind-altering substances, a stranger even to caffeine, tobacco, and alcohol. He feared what the medication might do to his personality. The alternative, though—ending up as an uncontaminated corpse—was also unappealing. He put aside his prejudices and started taking the meds. They did the job the doctor had predicted and one morning, about ten days later, Trevor woke up and felt as though he had "crossed a river from the dark, cold, clammy bank to its opposite, sunlit shore." The crossing itself, he says, was the easy part—the drugs did all the work. Learning to live on the sunny side was harder. He had to rethink what the changes meant to his life.

At the same time that his personal life was turning around, Trevor's ideas about his role as a naturalist and scientist began a slow swing through the points of a conceptual compass. The lodestone pulling the needle was his beloved lichens. Trevor had marked several lichen-rich locations near Edgewood for long-term observations. The seasonal changes he was seeing in the marked specimens didn't fit well with the typical categories that lichenologists employed to describe the differences between lichens. Trevor began to see new patterns that could be the source of testable hypotheses, a dozen of these patterns at first, then, as his perspectives began to widen, another dozen. Many of these hypotheses had to be phrased in language that used the vocabulary of ecology.

While he was wrestling with these profound personal and professional changes, Trevor partnered with three other naturalists to write a field guide to the lichens of British Columbia. He soon had the text for the book in hand, but he was not happy with it. "Too much emphasis," he says, "on how to identify lichens, not enough on why bother." He wondered how he could explore these new directions in print. Setting aside the field guide and making an arrangement with *Evansia*, the professional journal of the major North American association of lichenologists, he began a series of essays that he called "Twelve Readings on the Lichen Thallus." In these dozen essays— he is now adding a thirteenth—Trevor asks, in effect, what the scientific study of lichens might be like if the discipline had not been shackled with a century and a half of limiting assumptions about species and systematics.

❧

Trevor's "Readings on the Lichen Thallus" are on his Ways of Enlichenment web site. I printed copies before coming to Edgewood. After bedding down in one of the back rooms, I switch on the reading light, open my binder with the printouts, and look through them. Passages in the essays remind me of phrases I heard from Trevor this evening. "I no longer see the world—and lichens in particular—quite the way I saw it back in 1990," he says in the first essay. Calling lichens "fungi that have discovered agriculture" tips the mind toward the fungal component as the dominant partner. Reversing the slant by assigning priority to the algal component, although corrective in the short term, makes further concessions to received traditions about species. Both approaches obscure an essential fact: the two partners in a lichen cohabit a miniature, metaphorical ecosystem that acts in some respects like a singular species, in other respects like a distributed community.

The tension between species traditions and the reality of lichens leads to a problem, Trevor points out in one of his essays, with the received lichen names. Before Schwendener's discovery of their dual nature, lichens had good Linnaean binomial names. As more and more lichenologists came to accept the dual hypothesis, the botanical tradition in which they worked, the tradition that decreed binomials could only apply to singular species and not to conglomerations of species, began to shape the way they thought about lichen names. After struggling with this tension for many decades, the scientific community eventually enshrined, in its International Code of Botanical Nomenclature, the dictum that "names given to lichens apply to their fungal component." Every time we use a scientific name for a lichen—when we refer, for example, to the shrubby, chartreuse-colored wolf lichen as *Letharia vulpina*—there is an implicit asterisk on the scientific name reminding us that we are really using the fungal half of the lichen as a shorthand for a specific fungus and alga mix. This naming trick, letting one part stand for the whole, poses no problem so long as we assume a one-to-one relationship between a fungal partner and a named lichen. The assumption is not true, however: different lichens can and do share the same fungus. Assigning the Latin binomial to the fungal component, then, means that the lichen as a whole has, in essence, no scientific name. The organism's essential nature, its lichenness, is forced to the sidelines by a theology of nomenclature.

Trevor outlines eight ways that we can deal—or refuse to deal—with the lichenness of lichens. The approaches fall along a spectrum. At one end of the spectrum, we have the conventional species approach. It is

Wolf lichen, Letharia vulpina. Or at least the fungal part is Letharia vulpina. Photograph by Wendy Ansell.

not an unreasonable approach. Lichens, like plants, "grow in coordinated fashion, differentiate several tissue types, and pass through a succession of developmental stages culminating sooner or later in a reproductive phase." At the other extreme of the spectrum we have the view that lichens resemble ecosystems. The components—fungi, algae, and bacteria—come together to form an entity that is more than the sum of its parts. Some lichens achieve "a level of physiological integration and sophistication scarcely less 'perfect' than that within our own cells."

So what, then, is a lichen? Is it more like an organism or an ecosystem? Trevor wants both to be true. More than this, he says, both *must* be true: "Some of lichenology's most basic questions are likely to remain unanswered, perhaps even unasked, until such time as lichenologists learn to accord equal status—and research time—to lichens both as composite entities and as organisms." The first step in this direction, Trevor believes, is a shift to a systems perspective in which the parts and the features of a given lichen become pieces of a larger conversation. The lichen itself is always embedded in an environment and constantly responds to this environment. Faced with cascading and metabolically taxing cues from its environment, the main body of the lichen, the lichen thallus, "elaborates itself" through a series of responses to physiologic stress, eventually taking on the characteristics we associate with traditional lichen species. When we learn to read the decisions made by the growing lichen, the significance of the static lichen parts recedes and the focus shifts. A lichen becomes a story, not about the individual parts, but about the conversations between its parts.

From a systems perspective, every organism is a dynamic conversation. What makes lichens unique is that the conversation between the parts is much more front and center. In the case of a traditional species in a taxonomic group—*Homo sapiens* among the primates, for example—a lot of this conversation has sunk to an intracellular level. The organism's responses to the environment seem to be driven by acquired genetic and epigenetic coding. In the consortium that is a lichen, however, much of the conversation between its parts is carried on at a level above the cell, in a region where we are accustomed to assigning differences to nurture rather than nature. The decisions made by a lichen thallus feel, therefore, less coded and determined.

Trevor brings up the case of the edible horsehair lichen, *Bryoria fremontii*, to illustrate this loss of hard species determination among the lichens. The First Nations people of Western Canada, who used this lichen to make a vegetable/fruit pemmican, were careful to distinguish between an edible form of the lichen and a quite similar inedible form. Failure to heed this distinction could be fatal: the inedible form of this horsehair lichen accumulates vulpinic acid, the same toxin that gives wolf lichen its yellow cast and its name. (It was called "wolf lichen" because it was used to poison wolves.) Taxonomists, hewing to the native tradition, eventually came to designate the inedible and edible horsehairs as different species. Newer molecular work, however, suggests that the same fungus and alga are in both species. Going by the standard rules of nomenclature, the two hair lichens must be a single species. Going by traditional knowledge, buttressed by the later morphological work of lichenologists, the edible and inedible types of *Bryoria* are separate species. We like to think that problems such as these could be settled if only we had better genetic information about the organism. In this case, however, we don't even know where the line between the genetic code and its environmental expression should be drawn. The bold circles that we use to delineate species differences among the other animals and plants simply do not work for certain lichens. Key differences between lichens can pivot, not on the static genetic code, but on a dynamic conversation between the parts of the elaborating lichen.

The shift to metacellular conversations focuses new attention on the early developmental stages of lichens. Lichens in what Trevor calls their *pre-thallus* state make decisions that define the mature organism. Many lichens resynthesize from scratch at each new generation—the fungi divest themselves of their traditional photosynthetic partners and survive for a time in an amorphic, unlichenized phase. During this phase they are *paralichens*. In this paralichen stage the fungus may take on photosynthetic partners that it later rejects in favor of its mature partner. In theory, says Trevor, lichens should be able to remain in a paralichen state for years, even decades, before the right conditions trigger the appearance of the lichen thallus that is described in the field guides. Lichens, it seems, don't start out as lichens. They lichen themselves in the early stages of their development.

Trevor goes on in the "Readings on the Lichen Thallus" series to work out other implications of his switch to a system perspective. Approaching a lichen as a verb rather than as a noun affects, he says, how we look at lichen distribution patterns, the lichen internal carbon economy, the roles assigned to the various lichen structures, and more. I close the binder and turn off the light. In the silence of the Wells Gray night—tonight not even animal sounds intrude—two thoughts carry me into the oblivion of sleep.

The first thought is how far Trevor has departed from traditional ways of understanding lichens. Lichenologists have, for better or worse, come up with a standard script for fitting lichens into botanical and mycological frameworks. This species-but-not-really-a-species tactic may seem odd to those of us on the outside, but those who deal with the basics of lichen taxonomy, microbiology, and ecology aren't all that bothered by the contradictions. They have their canned answers to canned questions and these answers tell them that the contradictions are not serious. This sort of response is not bad behavior—when Thomas Kuhn did his analysis of the progress of science in his famous book, *The Structure of Scientific Revolutions*, he called these standard paradigms "normal science." Good science *is* normal science, at least most of the time. The assumptions we make are useful. They allow us to stop answering first questions over and over, letting us turn our attention to the implication of these assumptions, to get on with the game. The problem comes, Kuhn points out, when these assumptions begin to conceal points of data that don't fit the paradigm. The person who asks for a revision to a scientific paradigm on the basis of data overlooked by the paradigm's assumptions can appear dangerous, even deranged, to practitioners of the normal version of the science. He is, by definition, abnormal. When Trevor was telling me today about his essays, I asked him how they had been received by the lichen community. "Not that well," he said. "I haven't received any death threats, but some of the reactions have not been friendly."

The second of my Wells Gray night thoughts is how much lichens, when seen through Trevor's eyes, resemble other inhabitants of the boundary layer. Lichen species somehow manage to do most of what traditional species do, but they do it in an extracellular way, without the deep-coded, intracellular programs we usually associate with species definitions. At the same time, lichens can, when necessary, weaken the close bonds between their subcomponents and behave in ways that resemble a more distributed community of organisms. I wonder: If we had made less effort at the beginning of the twentieth century to shoehorn lichens into preconceived notions of species, would we have been so surprised when, at the end of the century, we started to encounter endosymbiotic cells, microbial-animal communities, superorganisms, and other denizens of the conceptual boundary layers between species and ecosystems? The lichens, it occurs to me, might have prepared us to accept the boundary conditions that have invaded our conceptual spaces in recent decades.

∾

I'm up early, in spite of the late night. Trevor is taking me on a walk into the forests across the pond from Edgewood. While waiting for him to show up, I wander along a few of the paths near the house. Trevor designed the house and had it built when he first moved here. Since then he has added a cabin for his guests. Behind the main house he has constructed mounded earth crossings that lead through a cattail swamp formed by an old beaver dam. Many of the paths around the buildings take the walker along gardens and terminate in group gathering points—low benches around campfire sites. In some ways the site seems more like a guest lodge than a private residence.

At breakfast I ask Trevor about Edgewood. He tells me about his dream that it will become an informal center for outdoor learning, a place where naturalists and others will gather to spend time in study and dialogue. The Clearwater Valley, he says, provides outstanding opportunities for research. Wildlife researchers knew this in the 1950s and 1960s. At that time, Wells Gray was home to more wildlife research than any other park in the BC Parks system. Today Wells Gray hosts little research. Trevor hopes to reverse this neglect. He has campaigned for Clearwater, the nearest town, to make its proximity to the park a part of its municipal identity. He has also donated part of Edgewood to the park system with the understanding that the province will establish an education and research center there. While waiting for BC Parks to make their move, he has been building up a network of "Edgewood types" who come for periods of time to bond with the park and contribute their perspectives to the environmental conversation.

The sun has burned away the morning frost by the time we cross over the swamp and enter the forest. Our first stop is at a small Douglas-fir with ribbons of colored tape tied to its branches. About twenty trees on his walking circuits, Trevor tells me, are marked this way. The marked branches haven't acquired lichen communities yet and he wants to learn which sets of environmental conditions promote lichen growth

Edgewood, guest house on left, main house in center. Photo by Jason Hollinger.

and which do not. The ribbons mark the various control and treatment patches. He carries small bottles of water and glucose on his hikes and sprays the marked branches. A yellow ribbon, for example, tells him that the branch gets a shot of glucose whenever he walks by.

As we hike deeper into the woods, the trees begin to display thick mantles of lichens. We begin to sense the presence of an active stegnon. None of the trees around us, however, appear to be more than a century old. I ask Trevor about this. Small patches of the Clearwater Valley, he says, have older trees, but a fire burned through the valley in 1926 and took out most of the older stands. The fire turned out to be a blessing—it made the valley unattractive to logging interests and permitted the province to secure the initial tracts that make up the half-million-hectare park.

We seem to be hiking cross-country, not following a path. When I mention this, Trevor points out the signs—the soil compression, nibbled limbs—that signal we are on a deer trail. "I lived here for twenty years before I started to follow deer trails. It took me more years to figure out the logic behind some of the local trails—why the deer turn this way instead of that. From our point of view the trails seem wandering and random, but from the deer's perspective the trails mark the lowest energy route between points of interest."

I've asked Trevor to show me the edible horsehair lichen that he wrote about in one of his essays. It was in the 1990s, while writing a popular article on hair lichens, he tells me, that he first began to work out his current ideas about lichen ecology. Next to a round meadow ("a filled-in glacial kettle," Trevor suggests) we find healthy clumps of *Bryoria* draped from several low branches. He pulls down a branch, takes out a hand lens, and shows me the signs that identify the lichen as edible horsehair. The stems are shinier than other horsehair lichens. The individual stems are thicker, more dimpled, grow longer, and branch less. "Supply it the right combination of wet and dry, dark and light, wind and calm, and edible horsehair can bulk up and become a key winter food for mountain caribou. Heavy rain causes carbohydrates to leach out all along the thallus, but these nutrients aren't lost to the lichen system. They are reabsorbed near the tips of the branching network." I ask if this nutrient package in the tips is why the First Nations peoples ate it. "It now looks as though lichens themselves are mostly indigestible to humans. What makes hair lichen useful as a food is the way it's prepared. First Nations people used long poles to twist it off the tree like candy floss. They would throw it in cooking pits with lots of edibles—especially berries and other sweeteners. After a few days the lichen would absorb nutrients that would otherwise be lost in the cooking process. It's the absorbed essence of berries, corms, and honey that makes lichen cakes—*wila* is what the interior Salish call them—good winter food. The licorice-like consistency of the cakes also made them appealing."

For the next while, our conversation turns to more abstract topics. Walking with Trevor must be what it would have been like to hike the Walden woods with Thoreau—a mixture of concrete observations and soaring flights of speculation. Trevor's hermit habits also resemble those of Thoreau. He likes to travel by foot and seldom gets far from his beloved Clearwater Valley. I ask him if isolation is a problem. "It can be. I'm finding it harder, for example, to write contemporary-sounding prose. I'm not in touch with the events that occupy other people. I get almost no news these days." He used to listen to radio, he says, but he unplugged it on the day after 9/11. He doesn't watch TV. He has a TV hooked up to a DVD player, but when he bought the television he told the salesperson that if he turned the dial and got a single station, he was returning the set. "News

Bryoria fremontii, *edible hair lichen, in Wells Gray Provincial Park.*

to me is where the snowline on the mountain is today, the moose tracks on the pond crossing, the honking of geese overhead. If there's anything else out there important for me to know, it will find its way to me."

Trevor is also occupied, as Thoreau was, by what it means to be an individual, what it means to live in, as he says, an "extra-centric" relation to one's society. "Healthy human societies, like ecosystems, depend on the proportionate functioning of unlike parts. Some people seem to believe that all of us should be more or less the same. But that's not what ecology teaches us. Our local salmon are an example. The Chinook salmon are spawning in Clearwater River right now, not far from here." Trevor turns his head and looks off in the distance, at what must be the location of the river. "Salmon, they say, always return to spawn and die in the stretch of stream they were born in. But that's not true. Every year a certain number of our spawners swim upstream, past the spawning grounds, to a low waterfall we call Bailey's Chutes. No salmon, to the best of my knowledge, has ever jumped the Chutes. Every year, though, there are salmon that try and there are tourists lined up along the stream bank to watch them try. It seems strange that the salmon would do this, but really it's not. Some day the rocks that form Bailey's Chutes will wear down and a salmon will make it over the top. If the old spawning grounds are lost, then a life that now seems pointless will suddenly have meaning."

I ask him if he is the salmon that tests the boundaries. "It's true that I'm drawn to do nonordinary things. These days I often find myself on the outside of science—and of society—looking in, saying 'Something's not quite right here, something's missing.'"

Ideas in which an entire process is . . . embraced
elude definition; only that which has no history is definable.
— Friedrich Nietzsche, *Zur Genealogie der Moral*

ᴏᴠ

The Trouble with Wilderness

Easter Monday, early morning, a steaming mug of sweet tea balanced in one hand, the other hand fumbling for car keys. I've got half an hour to get to Goldstream, one of British Columbia's provincial parks. Darren and Claudia Copley are meeting me there for a morning walk.

On the way to the park, I find myself grinning about what happened yesterday. My wife and I attend masses hosted by a local group of Franciscan friars. The celebrant for yesterday's Easter mass was the ninety-five-year-old Father Stan, recently transferred from full-time parish work and posted to the Victoria Friary. Father Stan is an uncomplicated man with a literal faith. He speaks, when he has to, in short, unnuanced sentences. During the Easter mass we repeated our baptismal vows. After the vows, Father Stan sprinkled the congregation with baptismal water. As he made his way down the center aisle of our small chapel, flinging water with the aspergillum to one side and the other as far as his frail arm could reach, he suddenly stopped and said in his loudest voice, "Even if the water doesn't touch you, you still have to repent."

The old priest, I think as I pull into the parking lot, could have been speaking about Goldstream Park. This thousand-acre jewel is a place where waters meet, waters that affect all of us on the southern end of Vancouver Island, whether we've felt the drops or not.

A few minutes later, Darren and Claudia's Smart Car pulls in next to mine. Darren is the president of the Victoria Natural History Society and Claudia edits the club's magazine. Every natural history concern in the Victoria area seems to intersect with the Copleys at some point. They are high-energy advocates in several local conservation efforts. For a number of years their lives twined with the story of Goldstream Park— Darren was employed by the park as an interpreter and manager and Claudia did seasonal work. In 2002, in a move that still has many British Columbia residents scratching their heads, the provincial government struck from its budget all of the park interpretation funds, the better part of a million dollars. Most of the BC Parks interpreters were underpaid, seasonal staff, so the move affected a large number of naturalists and educators. Some of these disjobbed interpreters have, as the Copleys, found other ways of being paid for doing what they love. Darren is now the environmental education officer for a local municipality and runs labs for the botany program at the University of Victoria. Claudia is the entomology collection manager at the Royal BC Museum.

As we greet each other, we find ourselves shouting over the background noise. Goldstream Park is bisected by the main north–south highway on Vancouver Island. The hum of wheels and the drone of motors is a constant undertone in areas of the park that lie below the road. Highway and park have a love/hate relationship: the din of traffic intrudes on the forest solitude, but proximity to the highway gives the park a prime location to retail its message about the interrelationships of natural systems.

Part of the Goldstream message is about salmon and their place in the coastal web of life. A series of linked lakes in the hills above the park run their waters into the ocean via Goldstream River. When the river reaches the park lands at the bottom of the valley, it slows down and transforms itself into prime spawning habitat for chum salmon. Chinook and coho pass through the chum spawning beds on their way upstream. Each autumn, tens of thousands of visitors come to watch the salmon lay their eggs and die. Another piece of the Goldstream message is about an endangered ecosystem. The Coastal Douglas-fir zone represented in the park occupies a small portion of the Pacific Northwest. Only scattered pockets of its old-growth forests remain.

The traffic noise fades as we make our way down one of the paths to the river. Claudia and Darren begin to talk about the history of the park. The First Nations people, they tell me, have used the park area for thousands of years. European civilization has occupied it for a mere century and a half. The first extended description of the site in European records—written by a colonial surveyor who worked at the park in 1852—reported that it was still a major fishing ground for the First Nations. Before the decade came to an end, Goldstream would begin a long tussle with Western civilization. For the next hundred years, the park area was constantly threatened by forces of development. The great reconstructors of the aboriginal lands of the Pacific Northwest have been forestry, mining, hydroelectric energy, agriculture, tourism, and housing. Agents of most of these forces turned their hungry gaze toward Goldstream at one time or another.

The first of the colonizing forces to notice Goldstream, the one that gave the park and river their current names, was mining. In the 1850s, the small European settlement in nearby Victoria found itself coping with wave after wave of prospectors, many of them drawn north from California's overworked gold fields by rumors of untapped mother lodes in Canada. Placer miners sifted the beds of Goldstream River in the 1850s, but the returns were low. When they began to dig along the banks of the river, however, the miners uncovered deposits of quartz that contained, they believed, enough gold to make extraction profitable. The most intense effort to establish a mining operation began in the fall of 1863, when the government took an interest in the project. Officials built roads and set up a mining camp. Prospectors cut down trees and ripped up the soil to reach gold-bearing veins in the bedrock. Plans were made to divert the river waters to sluice away soil and rock. One of the mining companies announced that it would build a quartz-crushing mill beside the river. But by the summer of 1864, not even a year after it had begun, the gold rush fizzled. Miners were drawn away to new diggings to the west and north. Desultory attempts to mine the area for other minerals would continue until the 1920s. During the 1940s, gravel would be scooped from a pit that is now inside the park boundaries. In the end, though, the mining sector would fail to prove up on its early claims, and Goldstream would survive the first attempt to cash in on its resources. Time has healed most of the park's gold-inflicted scars.

The second attempt to cash in on Goldstream arrived in the 1880s, when tourism discovered the park. A north–south rail line was constructed along the lower half of Vancouver Island, and Goldstream became a whistle-stop on the way out of Victoria. An Irish entrepreneur acquired a thousand acres of land in and around the current park and built a large hotel. For a round-trip fare of only twenty-five cents, a resident of Victoria could spend the day picnicking, hunting the local game, listening to a band concert, and drinking water that, the resort owner advertized, "smooths wrinkles of the old, gives health to the sick, beauty to the young, and wisdom to all." Warm summer weekends would find a thousand Victoria residents wandering the woods and fields of Goldstream. The development of an electric streetcar system in Victoria began to draw tourists to other locations, however, and by the end of World War I the Goldstream tourist boom was over. The hotel burned down in the

The old Goldstream Hotel, near Goldstream Park, 1886–1923. Image courtesy of the Royal BC Museum and Archives (C-03752).

1920s, and Goldstream, except for a prodigious slaughter of its wild animals, escaped the tourist assault intact.

The final threat to Goldstream came in the guise of a hydroelectric plant. In the 1890s, demand for electric power led to the construction of a hydroelectric generating station, the first on Canada's West Coast, at Goldstream. Within a few decades of the plant's construction, however, power lines from newer generating stations on the west side of the island reached Victoria. These western lines were soon joined by underwater trunks from the British Columbia mainland. To remain competitive, the hydroelectric installation at Goldstream needed to expand. The expansion threatened to restructure the Goldstream watershed. Fortunately for the river and the eventual park, the power company chose not to make further investments in their Goldstream enterprise. Use of the generating station declined, and the plant was mothballed in the 1950s.

Goldstream at the midpoint of the twentieth century had survived three major attempts on its life. The river still sheltered its salmon and significant tracts of the original forest stood tall. In the course of dodging the bullets of mining, tourism, and hydroelectric energy, the park and its watershed had come under the direct control of local government. Officials of the government began to look at the possibility of placing the region under some kind of long-term protection. The district ceded the lower area of the Goldstream watershed to the province for a provincial park in the late 1950s, retaining the upper area as a water supply region for Victoria and its suburbs. Park managers set about removing some of the new park's post-European intrusions. At the same time they upgraded and extended visitor services.

Darren, Claudia, and I arrive at the gravel path along the river. No one else is here today—the main visitor season is still more than a month away. The path meanders among some of the largest trees in the region. The red cedars, many of them more than six centuries old, are spectacular, with trunks nearly two meters in diameter and the lowest branches far above our heads. They are here because the Goldstream River provides subsoil water. The river also contributes an abundance of nitrogen. In the years before the colonists drove the larger mammals away, the huge salmon runs lured bears to the river. The bears dragged salmon carcasses into the woods and the decomposing fish donated their nitrogen reserves to the soil around the trees. The ages of trees that lie within fifty meters of a salmon stream, researchers have learned, do not correlate well with their sizes. Salmon streams are steroids for tree growth.

Several areas next to the path have been cordoned off by a rail fence in recent years. Like grown siblings returning to a home where they had once lived, the Copleys wander from one fence to another, pointing out to each other how the various plants have responded to protection. "When I worked here, we discovered the importance of restricted access by accident," says Darren. "We used to let people wander along the lower reaches of the river and into the estuary. One year the riverside path was damaged by floods. The park didn't have the money to repair it, so we decommissioned the trail and designated the area as a quiet zone. That year fifty eagles showed up to feast on dying salmon. Before that we had been lucky if we saw two or three in a season. A few years later a bear started hanging around and the estuary had to be closed off to protect the bear and the visitors. Eagle numbers jumped to more than two hundred that fall. Native plants began to thrive in the estuary—dodder, as-

ter, angelica. We learned from these events that the estuary needed to be people-free. A remotely controlled camera allows visitors to see what is happening without disturbing the plants and wildlife." As we cross a small footbridge, Claudia points out where the river used to flow. "About ten years ago," she says, "a flood shifted the course of the river to where it is now." I look at where she is pointing, but the shrubby vegetation resembles all the other stretches of riverbank. The rapid responses of the ecosystem were learned

Darren Copley at Goldstream Park.

long before people began to manage the park. An intact ecosystem, like a healthy organism, knows how to make its own repairs.

As we walk along the river, our talk turns to the park's salmon. I've seen the autumn runs. So many salmon crowd the lower reaches of the river that they jostle each other for space. While the number of chum salmon returning to breed at Goldstream has remained high, the salmon breeds most sought after as food and game, the coho and chinook, have seen precipitous declines. "Some of the First Nations still fish at Goldstream, don't they?" I ask.

"Yes," says Darren. "Five bands still have fishing rights here. Visitors sometimes resent it when they see the bands fishing the river, but the overall First Nations impact is small. If you need to take salmon for food, the best time is when they enter rivers. We can count the fish here and understand the impact of the choices we make. When the fish return to the ocean, our lack of knowledge interferes. How do we know when we are overfishing the ocean populations?"

We turn toward a car bridge that spans the river. A loud whistle sounds. It reminds me of a referee trying to be heard over the noise of a basketball game. "A varied thrush," says Darren. "I've heard the sound described as an ethereal trill. The river paths are some of the best areas in Goldstream to watch for birds." He steps off the path and gently turns a log. Insects and spiders flee from the light. "Red-backed salamanders are common in the park. When I was working here, I would often find them under this log." He rolls the log back to where it was. I'm starting to hear Darren's interpreter voice. Thousands of children have carried home from Goldstream a piece of Darren's enthusiasm. "Do you miss working with children?" I ask.

"Yes and no. In recent years I've come to realize how important it is to put people in contact with conservation issues at the time they are making career decisions. When people learn to love a park as a child, they can become adults who love it to death, who want to come here to hike, camp, walk their dogs, ride their horses. Sometimes the best thing we can do for a protected area is simply to protect it. Instead, we put in parking lots, washrooms, trails, then spend all of our time managing the crowds."

Small seasonal waterfall, early spring, Goldstream Park.

We cross the bridge and descend to an area on the far bank, stopping in front of a cliff draped in dripping mosses and maidenhair ferns. A rivulet cascades down the rocks and runs into a channel that joins the river. If Goldstream has a chapel, this is it. We stand in silence for a while, taking in the scene.

"Did experiences when you were young set the two of you on your career paths?" I ask.

"Not in my case," says Darren. "I did a degree in biology, but I was planning on going into medicine. A friend in California persuaded me to attend a conference on park interpretation. At the conference, I realized that this was what I really wanted. After I graduated from the University of Victoria, I started doing bird censuses and wildlife habitat consulting. Claudia and I met when I volunteered to help with some birding field trips at the university."

"I imprinted on natural systems when I was young," says Claudia. "My parents were poor. We couldn't afford to buy a lot of exotic nursery plants, so we had a number of native plants in our garden. We were surrounded by wild spaces waiting to be explored. But my real love was insects. I adored bugs, even when I was a little girl. I collected them, kept them as pets. When I went to university, I decided to follow this interest and study entomology."

We recross the bridge, return to our cars, and drive to the campgrounds along the upper areas of Goldstream River. Soon we are threading single file along a narrow path leading up a ridge. Thirty meters below us the river plunges down the hill in a series of rapids and waterfalls. As we move away from the river channel, the vegetation alters in subtle steps. Claudia starts seeing insects that weren't in the lower areas of the park. A strange fly lands on a salal leaf. "One of the Dolichopodidae," she says, "the long-legged flies." Darren turns up some lethargic banana slugs hiding under logs along the trail. Birds pip and cheep in the canopy, and Darren calls out their names. Here and there are the early blooms of Lyall's anemone, each flower a child's stubby white fingers cupped around a ball of green. At one bend in the path, we come upon a rib cage of hemlock roots that once surrounded a nurse log.

We turn toward the parking area, heading back to where we left our cars. As we hike though the campground, we are eyed by a young raccoon in the crotch of a tree. A red squirrel scolds us from the safety of a high branch. "What's going to happen to Goldstream?" I ask.

Darren shakes his head. "I don't know. It's a provincial park, and that's a plus. But right now no one is quite sure what that means. Changes were happening to the parks long before cuts to the interpretation budget forced us to move on. Many of the park services had been handed over to contractors. I was employed by one of these contractors during the years that I was here. The person I initially worked for had been an employee of the park system, and his goals were in line with traditional park values. But it was tough for him to make the interpretation programs work. Budgets were being shaved every year. Eventually a new contractor came in and the work environment became unfriendly. When my employer came to the park to see how operations were going, he would pull his Hummer into the stall beside my Smart Car. That's when I knew I had no future at Goldstream."

When we get to the parking area, Claudia opens the hatch door at the back of their tiny car and hands me a thick ream of paper. It's a background paper on Goldstream that the Copleys wrote for teachers who bring their students to the park. The paper, I later discover, is the only serious attempt to write a natural history of the park. I leaf through the pages as Darren and Claudia's car pulls away. A line near the end of the manuscript catches my eye: "Except for road, hydro line, railway right-of-way, and the gravel pit, the effect of humans on vegetation in Goldstream Provincial Park has been relatively limited. This has led to a fortuitous situation whereby trees close to seven hundred years old are found in close proximity to a large urban center like Victoria."

I look around me. We left our cars just outside the park, at the entrance to the campgrounds. Across the road is an imposing pub that was built on the site of the old Goldstream Hotel. Heavy-duty pickups follow each other in close procession along the road next to the pub, most of them no doubt owned by the residents of the new developments hugging the edge of the park. Power and utility lines crisscross overhead. A few meters away, however, at the park border, all of this busyness stops, and the visitor enters a tableau of an ancient ecosystem that has dominated the southern tip of Vancouver Island for many millennia. The border seems tenuous, undefended. That this boundary even exists, however, is due to an astounding run of luck.

I doubt that Father Stan would call it luck. A simple faith that sees repentance in a drop of baptismal water would find a miracle in the preservation of Goldstream Park.

❧

Until the twentieth century, the preservation of any wilderness depended largely on the same luck/miracle that saved Goldstream Park. Today, chance is less of a factor. We plan and carry out the preservation of wilderness lands. Tens of thousands of tracts of North American land have been set aside, many of them under the guidance of specific preservation goals.

To justify modern preservation efforts, we often make use of words and meanings that did not exist a hundred years ago. Several decades of regular use have given the new vocabulary a familiar feel. Some of it, though, has yet to settle in. Conservation words that are employed with full transparency by one group are hedged with scare quotes by another. Much is at stake in the battle for these words. In this last chapter, we will boot the search for boundary layers to more conceptual level and look at borderlands, not in our natural systems, but in our conversations about natural systems.

Any discussion about the vocabulary of land preservation brings us into contact, sooner or later, with Aldo Leopold. Leopold spent his life straddling several of the preservation movement's most important conceptual boundaries. In 1887, the year he was born to a well-to-do family in Eastern Iowa, the frontier of European settlement in North America was still in view. His German grandparents had watched the line of settlement ferry across the Mississippi and spread out across the tallgrass prairies of the Midwest. The effects of this settlement were still light on the land when Leopold was a boy. The outdoorsy lad had easy access to pockets of undeveloped wilderness. Day after day he wandered the woods and wetlands near his home, learning to recognize plants and animals, watching changes in the landscape, making notes. When he was old enough, he hunted. Leopold's predation was not the smash-and-grab of many of the pioneers. Hunting trips with his father were lessons in a moral understanding of nature. The boy learned that not all species of birds were taken, not all seasons were the right times for hunting.

Leopold had just entered his teens when William McKinley was assassinated and Theodore Roosevelt became the youngest-ever American president. Among the trust-busting values that Roosevelt brought to the White House was a belief that the American people should hold back sections of the American landscape from commercial conscription. When Roosevelt began his term as president, the major set-aside lands—mostly in Wyoming's Yellowstone region and California's Yosemite Valley—were those that railroad companies thought they could make money from. He expanded these lands in giant leaps. By the time Roosevelt left office, almost a million square kilometers of the United States had been reserved as parks, forests, and national monuments.

Roosevelt's newly reserved lands were not, however, protected wildernesses. They were working lands that were expected to provide certain raw materials for the expanding American economy. The United States Forest Service was established to manage these lands. Roosevelt's friend Gifford Pinchot became chief forester, and the wealthy Pinchot family helped endow the Yale Forest School, America's first graduate program in forestry. In his late teens, Leopold traveled east, first to enroll in a preparatory school, then to complete the program in forestry at the new Yale school. Leopold moved seamlessly from his Yale studies into a position with the new Forest Service. In 1909, he was assigned to his first job: an assistant in the Arizona Territory's Apache National Forest.

Forest Assistant Aldo Leopold at the Apache National Forest. Image courtesy of the Forest History Society, Durham, NC (image FHS4408).

The work of the Forest Service in these early years—and therefore most of Leopold's work—was arranging contracts for grazing and logging on public lands. The scale of what was placed in Leopold's hands impressed the young man. He wrote home to his mother about "millions of acres, billions of feet of timber, all vast amounts of capital. . . . It's fun to twiddle them around in your fingers." A few years into his new job, Leopold was leveled by a kidney infection. He read a lot during his months of convalescence, and what he read expanded Leopold's view of what his job was about. He wrote to his colleagues in the Forest Service that, "after many days of much riding down among thickets of detail and box canyons of routine, it sometimes profits a man to top out on the high ridge . . . and to take a look around."

Leopold's high ground gave him better perspective on the wild animals on Forest Service lands. Management of game was becoming a significant public issue in the second decade of the twentieth century. Game protection associations were being organized and several states had passed laws to restrict hunting. Leopold, tracking with these new trends, began to see a dimension to the national forests that his colleagues had overlooked. The forestry he had learned at Yale had not paid much attention to the game animals on the lands and forests. The job of the Forest Service, he came to believe, was to manage more than just grass and timber resources. Its vision had to encompass the whole land. In the long run, he would argue, there was "no such thing as forestry, no such thing as game management." The only reality was "an intelligent respect for, and adjustment to, the inherent tendency of land to produce life." With his health returning in fits and starts, Leopold traveled around Arizona and New Mexico to evangelize for the establishment of local game protection groups. He encouraged the new groups to unite into regional associations. During World War I, Leopold took a break from the Forest Service to work on city and state political issues that affected conservation efforts. After the war he returned to the Forest Service as one of the managers of the Southwestern District.

By the early 1920s, Leopold had taken tentative steps away from the assumptions of Rooseveltian conservation that had shaped his early years. He started to use the word *ecology* in his writings and to make his first forays into issues that would occupy the second half of his life.

How, he asked, can people live in a way that acknowledges and respects the web of nonhuman life that occupies the same land? His early steps in this new direction did not take him far, however. Leopold was still in the grip of a utilitarian approach to natural systems that devalued certain parts of the environment in favor of other parts. He pressed for the suppression of nongame wildlife in *The Pine Cone*, a newsletter he edited (and largely authored) for the game protection associations, appealing for "a reduction in the predatory animal population. . . . The wolves, lions, coyotes, bob-cats, foxes, skunks, and other varmints . . . continue to thrive and their reduction can be accomplished only by means of a practical, vigorous, and comprehensive, plan of action." The varmint reduction campaign was an unfortunate success: during Leopold's tenure in the Southwest, many of the local predator species would be hunted, trapped, and poisoned to near extinction. His overall journey, though, was leading him away from such intrusive management. Leopold was starting to see the importance of tempering human impact on *all* ecosystem components.

His writings in these years began to emphasize the importance of retaining tracts of land as roadless wildernesses. In 1922, he proposed to his Forest Service superiors that a half million acres in west-central New Mexico, the lands around the headwaters of the Gila River, be set aside as a wilderness preserve. He defined wilderness as "a continuous stretch of country preserved in its natural state, open to lawful hunting and fishing, big enough to absorb a two weeks' pack trip, and kept devoid of roads, artificial trails, cottages, or other works of man." Leopold submitted the proposal to the Forest Service. A year later, the service designated the headwater lands as the Gila Wilderness Area. Gila became the first land reserve in North America, arguably the first land reserve in the world, to be tagged with a term—*wilderness*—that recognized the intrinsic value of land in a natural state.

In 1924, Leopold accepted a job with the service's Forest Products Laboratory. He left his beloved New Mexico and moved his southwestern wife and their growing family to a new home in Madison, Wisconsin. Leopold would remain in Wisconsin for the rest of his life. The state had few areas that could be candidates for wilderness designation, but the idea of wilderness was never far from Leopold's thoughts. Ten years after moving to Wisconsin, he would join with seven others to found an advocacy group, The Wilderness Society. In the last decade of his life, with the government preoccupied with fighting the Great Depression and World War II, not much could be done about wilderness preservation, but in the thirty years following the war, Leopold's society would become a significant player in the move to reclassify a hundred million acres of government lands as reserved wilderness.

∾

Leopold and others who use the term *wilderness* to divide one part of the natural world from another have boarded a locomotive that pulls a number of conceptual rail cars. *Nature,* the more comprehensive term that *wilderness* refines, drags behind it an even longer and more complex train. When we use these two terms to talk about places such as Goldstream Park, we employ terms that are *social constructs.*

Social constructs behave in a peculiar way. Most nouns, we tend to think, are pointers to what is outside us. They are names that stand for the actions, things, and qualities that populate our world. Some words, though, seem to have a more inward function. They serve to glue together the social frameworks that support our lives, giving us a place to stand when we look outward. The great majority of the nouns in any language are, of course, amalgams of the two sides, conjunctions of what we experience as the *out there,* the real world, and how we want to organize our personal and social worlds. Certain terms, though, seem to lean more to the inside, and it is these words, the ones that call special attention to the inner relationships that they forge and maintain, that we most easily recognize as social constructs. The attachments of these social constructs to inner frameworks can be so tight, in fact, that the words become difficult to map onto the outside world of things and events. Take the terms *democracy, intelligence,* and *salvation.* Words such as these convey their intended meanings only to those who are privy to a shared framework of personal and community meaning.

Some social constructs, however, have just the opposite problem. They map too readily onto the outside world—so readily that we tend to forget that they are social constructions. A number of these outward-pointing words play important roles in scientific discourse. When we think about words such as *time, gravity,* and *disease,* we feel that what is described by these words has been discovered rather than invented. The words have, we might say, a high *thingness index* that grates against the idea that they are defined in significant ways by their social and intellectual contexts.

In *The Structure of Scientific Revolutions,* the book I mentioned earlier, Thomas Kuhn calls attention to the way these outward-pointing but socially charged scientific terms lead us into confusion. He begins by defining temporal scientific frameworks, which he calls *paradigms,* and describing how these paradigms encompass long periods of normal science. On the rare occasion when a new paradigm replaces an old one (e.g., the sun-centered Copernican view of the solar system banishes the earth-centered Ptolemaic view), it "incorporates much of the vocabulary and apparatus . . . that the traditional paradigm had previously employed." The arrival of this old baggage in the new paradigm creates a problem. The two paradigms, the old and the new, seldom employ these transferred terms in exactly the same way. This subtle lack of correspondence in the meaning of the terms causes those who work inside competing paradigms to misunderstand each other.

In Kuhn's story about paradigm change, the paradigms "practice their trade in different worlds," and the thinkers who move from one paradigm to another seldom make the transition "a step at a time, forced by logic and neutral experience." The transition between a paradigm and its successor requires, for most of those who have grown up inside the old paradigm, a sort of conversion. This conversion tends to scour away the intellectual lines connecting words that have traveled across paradigm boundaries. It is the social components of these far-traveling words that contribute to the ensuing confusion. A term gets stripped of its old social connections and switched into the new paradigm on the basis of some perceived similarity between the term's objective referent—its "out there-ness"—within the two paradigms. Once it has been transferred from the old paradigm, the word reattaches to different social components in its new paradigm. It becomes, in effect, a new word, but it does this without losing the shape of the old word.

Discussions of word behavior at this level can be a bit abstract. Let's pause to look at a pair of words that have caused confusion when they shifted their paradigms: *race* and *species*. The word *race* attached itself in the seventeenth and eighteenth centuries to regional divisions of humankind. It resettled groups of people into an intellectual framework that licensed the exploitation of one race by another. Certain obvious biological markers, skin tones in particular, became part of the term's meaning. To the visible markers identifying people of a given race, Europeans would silently append negative judgments such as "lazy," "deceptive," and "subintellectual." In the nineteenth century, when social attitudes toward these assumptions began to shift, certain connotations of the terms used to describe members of other races became harder to tolerate. At this point the whole intellectual construct behind the word *race* could have—probably should have—been scuppered. Instead, we rinsed the centuries of prejudicial dirt from the word and brought it into a new social paradigm that condemned the attitudes that had given rise to the term in the old paradigm. The term *race* attached itself to new objects, objects such as ethnicity and statistical genomic patterns. Speakers were encouraged to believe that they could talk about African and Asian races without invoking the sordid attitudes that were packaged with the original meaning. The success of this transfer is open to question, however. Many now believe that we cannot correlate the modern word with anything objective. When we use the term *race*, even in scientific studies, we import, subconsciously and dangerously, a classification that still depends on the term's older, oppressive context. Dorothy Roberts argues for this position in her 2011 book *Fatal Invention*. Race, she says, "is a political system that governs people by sorting them into social groupings based on invented biological demarcations. . . . Race is not a biological category that is politically charged. It is a political category that has been disguised as a biological one."

A second example of a word that led to confusion when it was frog-marched across paradigm boundaries is *species*. The word acquired its original meaning within an older scientific and theological paradigm. The older framework employed the term to stress the uniqueness and separateness of the different objects of God's creation. When natural philosophers made the transition to the evolutionary paradigm, the word was retained, its older associations jettisoned, and new referents assigned. But in the new paradigm, with organisms in constant meta- morphosis over geologic time, finding slices of organic consistency that could fill the role of what were once immutable species proved to be more difficult than the early evolutionists imagined. Two dozen ways of defining species within the new paradigm have been proposed; two dozen have been found wanting. By now it has become clear that there will never be a wholly satisfactory way of handling the word *species* in the new paradigm. The high thingness index of the word conceals how deeply the term is embedded in the social constructions of its source paradigm.

Many of the social constructs that have been developed over the last century in order to help us think about our placement in the natural world have this same high thingness index. These include some of the key terms that Leopold and other environmental scientists have applied to places like Goldstream. The words have an objective feel that hides the fact that they are social constructions. Take the term *nature*. It's hard to imagine a more out-there word. We often use it in phrases such as "na- ture versus nurture" that underline its separateness from the social world. But a glance at the word's history uncovers a long and strong association between this term and a series of social and intellectual frameworks.

The word *nature* in English derives much of its meaning from its role as a translation for the Greek word *physis*. When classical writers such as Aristotle used *physis*, the image behind their word lacked the out-there quality that *nature* has for us. The Greek word lies closer to the other meaning of *nature* in English: nature as essence, the sense of the word *nature* that is on display when we talk about "natural instincts" or "inner nature."* In the second book of his *Physics*, Aristotle contrasts things that display intelligent, purposeful behavior with elements of the world that are the result of artifice. A wooden bed, Aristotle points out, is artificial. It is not its own cause. It is a caused thing, crafted by some being capable

---

*The title of David Suzuki's popular CBC program *The Nature of Things* is a play on two of the meanings of nature—nature as the natural world, the subject of most of the broadcasts in the series, and nature as the characteristics that make something what it is.

of intentional change. The bed doesn't exhibit growth, reproduction, adaptation, or any other characteristics of a living being. A bed may, however, be made out of materials, such as trees, that *are* living, that are guided by inner purpose. If you dig up the soil and plant a four-poster, Aristotle says, you might, providing some part of the wood had retained its life principle (soul), end up with a new tree; you would never, however, grow a new four-poster. In contrast to an artificial thing such as a bed, a natural being has "within itself a principle of motion and stationariness." It can reproduce, act with intelligent purpose, cause movement. Natural elements include, besides people and plants and animals, the elemental parts of the world, such as fire, earth, air, and water. The list of living beings includes the world itself, the whole we commonly call Nature.

Lumping nature itself with other living beings leads Aristotle to explain motion in nature as a kind of intelligent purpose. This explanation is the one aspect of Aristotle's physics that high school graduates tend to know something about. When science teachers cover the unit on Newton's laws of motion, they often contrast Newton's explanations with those provided by Aristotle. Dropped balls fall to the earth, says Newton, because the earth attracts them by gravitational pull. Both the earth and the balls are passive, driven by outside mechanical laws. Newton's philosophy of nature replaced an Aristotelian framework that had dominated the Middle Ages. Aristotle, the high school teacher goes on to explain, believed that dropped balls fall to the earth because they *want* to go there. This pronouncement is usually followed by a pause for the class to laugh at how silly Aristotle's view is. But Aristotle only looks silly because the teacher and the students share an assumption that Aristotle didn't. They assume that nature is passive and inanimate. If you replace this assumption with the belief that nature is more like a person, then the alternate explanations of physical processes make more sense. Aristotle's ball would have been composed of intelligent elemental materials (e.g., earth) whose basic goal was to sink, to join other bits of earth in the lowest position of the planetary system that they can reach.

The response of the teacher and the class is a signal that the word *nature* has a strong social component, both in Aristotle's ancient paradigm and in our own. But how, if we started out the Western tradition of science by thinking that nature was more like a person, did we get to the place where we are today, the place where we contrast nature with people and their societies? Let's follow, for a moment, the steps that lead from the Greeks to us. For convenience, I'll mark out five of them.

The first step is the Aristotelian view of nature. The next move toward the modern view, step two, happened when Greek philosophy was taken up by the Christian church. The church is often seen as a passive conduit of Greek ideas into the modern world. In the case of the Greek view of nature, however, the church added an important element to its classical heritage: it brought Semitic views of a creator God into Western thought. This new element reinforced, in some ways, the Greek view of nature. The same God who created people in his image also reproduced himself in nature. Natural phenomena came to be seen, the saying goes, as a "glove on the hand of God." In other ways, however, the change made to Aristotle's view by the theologians of the church diverted the classical stream of ideas into a new channel. To the Greek philosophers, the animate principle of nature was inside nature. The theologians moved the bearer of agency outside of nature. Not far outside—at the height of the Renaissance, the passion for classical teaching led many thinkers to an almost animistic view. The vital principle that is God was reflected, they believed, in even the most inanimate aspects of nature. The Anglican theologian Richard Hooker, writing at the end of the sixteenth century, assured us that "those things which nature is said to do, are by divine art performed, using nature as an instrument." Everything done by "things natural which are not in the number of voluntary agents . . . proceedeth originally from some such agent, as knoweth, appointeth, holdeth up, and even actually frameth the same." Shakespeare, Hooker's contemporary, found nature so filled with agency that it could respond to, not only the direct plans of the divine, but also the less powerful intentions of God's representatives. The powers of nature could bend to the will of a banished Prospero and echo the moods of a deposed King Lear.

The external placement of this animating God would, within a century of Hooker and Shakespeare, open the door to a new view of nature. For the third step in the transformation of the term *nature*, we turn to R. G. Collingwood. I discovered Collingwood's writings in the same years in which the University of Chicago's Richard McKeon was knocking into my head the texts of Aristotle. Collingwood's idealist leanings turned out

---

**FIVE STEPS IN THE DEVELOPMENT OF THE
WESTERN CONCEPT OF NATURE**

Step 1: *Aristotelian nature.* Nature and some of nature's elements are living
beings. Nature is analogous to mind.

Step 2: *Christian nature.* The mind present in nature is the mind of God.
Nature is a glove on the hand of God.

Step 3: *Late Renaissance nature.* Nature is a regular system created by God.
Having no internal agency, it is analogous to a machine.

Step 4: *Enlightenment nature.* God withdraws. Nature is part of a universe with
regular laws. The laws may have ultimate divine or natural sources,
but they are unbreakable within the sphere of nature.

Step 5: *Romantic nature.* Nature is a complex, dynamic, self-regulating entity.
Nature is analogous to a process.

---

to be a good foil for McKeon's pragmatism. In Collingwood's book *The
Idea of Nature*, published after the end of his sadly short life, he outlines
the cosmological systems that have contributed to the modern understanding of nature. The Greek view of nature, Collingwood writes, was
"based on the principle that the world of nature is saturated or permeated
by mind. Greek thinkers regarded the presence of mind in nature as the
source of . . . regularity or orderliness in the natural world." Over the
next millennium and a half the church shoehorned the Greek view into
a Christian theological framework. Nature retained its agency, but the
agency was now identified as the sometimes hidden, sometimes revealed,
mind of God. Collingwood detects a sudden change to this Christian-
ized Greek view in the late Renaissance, during the early expressions of
modern scientific thought. Writers such as Nicolaus Copernicus, Francis
Bacon, and Giordano Bruno, he points out, began to switch analogies.
Printing presses, clocks, and other mechanical devices were showing up
all over Europe, and the early scientists latched on to these new devices
to explain the workings of nature. In adopting these mechanical analogies, they subtly altered the meaning of the word *nature*. The regularities
of nature were no longer due to an involved intelligence that manipulated every event. They were due, instead, to passive laws established
by an external agent, a wise but distant creator. What was once a simple
glove on the hand of God started to look more like a complex prosthetic

arm of God. The thinkers of the late Renaissance began to believe that workings of the divine mechanical arm, the processes of nature, could be studied on their own. We find an increasing alienation between God and nature both in the Cartesianism of the European continent and the streams of natural philosophy that flowed from the Newtonian synthesis in Britain.

Placing God outside of nature led, some two centuries later, to the fourth step in the journey: the complete withdrawal of God. The machine-like operations of nature that captivated the imaginations of seventeenth-century thinkers gradually edged an active God from the scientific picture. Thinkers reading essays about nature no longer expected to see references to divine causality. In the operations of the social world, however, God's hand still filled the glove. Kings and queens continued to channel divine authority. In the late eighteenth century, Enlightenment thinkers began to argue that the machine analogy that had worked so well for nature also applied to God's work with people and nations. Deists went so far as to argue that the God who designed and built the universe was no longer needed to explain anything after the initial creation. The pious Blaise Pascal complained that the philosopher Descartes "wanted to avoid God everywhere in his philosophy, but he was forced to allow him a flick of the finger to start the world moving; after that he had no more use for him." As the chains of explanation based on social and historical laws lengthened, the idea of God gradu- ally withdrew from the detail of the world. God became, for more and more European intellectuals, a hypothesis that was no longer relevant to either nature or society. Direct contact with the divine was increasingly relegated to a personal, inner, spiritual world that was segregated from the realm of rational explanation. Pascal may have complained about the trend evident in the writings of the older Descartes, but he was as captive to the shift in ideas as the rest of his seventeenth-century compatriots. On a piece of paper that a servant of Pascal found sewn into his dead master's shirt, the scientist and philosopher described a mystical vision that had seized him on the evening of November 23, 1654. "FIRE," he wrote, had blazed from the personal "God of Abraham, God of Isaac, God of Jacob." The fire, the note went on to say, had not come from "the God of the philosophers and the scholars." That God had gone on a trip and abandoned the world to its own devices. Pascal had to look inside himself to find what had been an external reality for his parents and grandparents.

The withdrawing agency of God left behind it a divided world. How did the natural world and the other world, the world of people and society, connect to each other? They each had their laws, but how did the two sets of laws interact? In the Greek view, the two parties had an innate unity—both were living organisms. In medieval cosmology, they were united by an active divinity who had decreed both sets of laws. In the early stages of the scientific revolution, the machine analogy of nature distanced God from nature, but the retreating divine was still invoked to unify the natural and social world. By the early nineteenth century, however, even this small link had snapped. For the capitalists of the industrial revolution, who were beginning to transform large swaths of the natural world into economic tokens, nature was a passive partner, with no vestige of the kinds of agency found in the social world. Nature became a resource, seemingly infinite, that could be farmed, mined, dammed, paved, and polluted.

Industrial expansion triggered, by its thoughtless rapacity, an opposition to step-four Enlightenment ideas about nature. We collect the many aspects of this reaction under the heading of Romanticism. The Romantic revolt from Enlightenment ideas at the end of the eighteenth century did not, in its first decades, directly address the problems raised by an active human agency and its consumption of passive natural resources, but it did lay the groundwork for a later rethinking of these problems. At the heart of the Romantic vision was a new analogy. When the Greeks looked at nature, they saw mind. When the early Western scientists looked at nature, they saw a machine. The Romantics looked around them and saw *process*.

The vision of process cultivated by early Romantic thinkers was, like all visions in their early stages, uncomfortable with too much detail, and Enlightenment science was offering up mind-numbing volumes of detail during the nineteenth century. To keep from drowning in this flood of external data, Romantic thinkers tended to focus on human experiences that were more difficult to reduce to dead facts. They became, not scientists, but philosophers, musicians, poets, novelists, and mystics. When they did wander into the natural sciences, the results of these incursions were not always happy. The philosopher Hegel was a bone-deep Romantic, and his dialectical philosophy stands as one of the earliest theoretical depictions of the new Romantic view of process. But when he applied his dialectic to the contemporary dialogues of natural science—as in the philosophy of nature section of his *Encyclopedia*—he walked off the end of a pier into water that was, most would agree, over his head.

Other nineteenth-century figures had more success in introducing Romantic process into a study of the natural world. Alexander von Humboldt, as we noted earlier, tried to turn the attention of natural scientists away from a dull catalog of species toward a study of ecological dynamism. The larger union of these dynamisms in what Humboldt called *cosmos* did not endure, but his message about process in nature hung around long enough to influence the birth of environmental science. The New England transcendentalists, the Americans who first adopted the Romantic gospel, confined most of their work on natural systems to mystical and philosophical musings. But Henry David Thoreau, especially in the last two decades of his life, carried transcendentalist ideas into a more detailed study of the natural world. Later in the nineteenth century, John Burroughs and John Muir blended serious natural history with Romantic intuition. Their writings were popular with the general public, less so with scientists.

The first serious meeting of the minds between the Romantic process metaphor and the assumptions of the expanding natural sciences arrived with the new environmental sciences of the late nineteenth century. The early ecologists took the dynamism revealed by the new view of evolution and used it to construct complex narratives of natural change. Not all ecologists drew the same conclusions from the new revelation of process. Ecology, as we noted in an earlier chapter, has always been a somewhat ambivalent science. Analysis of small processes does not always point to Process writ large. But a significant minority of ecologists—in some decades even a majority—have been willing to address wider issues. The organicism of Frederic Clements, as noted earlier, was the gold standard of American ecology for the first third of the twentieth century. In the last third of the century, James Lovelock's

Gaia hypothesis seeded environmentalism with a variously interpreted vision of deep process.

∾

The struggle between Enlightenment and Romantic metaphors of nature emerges with particular clarity in the wilderness movement of the twentieth century. The word *wilderness*, like the word *nature*, is a social construct with a high thingness index. Those who employ the word *wilderness* would like us to think that they are talking about undeveloped tracts of land—what Darwin's friend Thomas Huxley called, in the diary of his four-year voyage on HMS *Rattlesnake*, "the grand untrodden forest." The word has an inside dimension, however. Advocates of wilderness preservation are also deploying Romantic metaphors of nature. Wilderness areas, they say, are places where nature is allowed to be process, where processes that we do not fully comprehend have a protected home. We can't always be certain, when we hear the word *wilderness*, which side of the inside/outside line we are on. Is wilderness something we encounter, or is it an idea that we use to organize our way of looking at the world?

This ambivalence we find in the word *wilderness* forms a backdrop to the life of Aldo Leopold. Nineteenth-century descriptions of conservation lands tended to be framed in utilitarian terms. The set-aside parcels were places that were *conserved*, not used up all at once, but their ultimate fate was still bound up with economic need. At the turn of the twentieth century, the notion of *preservation*—setting aside land to *not* be developed—began to take hold. John Muir's vision of Yosemite as a cathedral for the worship of nature, for example, helped to convince Roosevelt and the federal government that its mountains should be housed in a national park. When Aldo Leopold pressed for the Gila lands to be set aside as wilderness, however, he reverted to the earlier utilitarian language. The headwaters, he said, would become a place for wilderness hunting and camping. He would later expand his understanding of wilderness to take in scientific goals. Wildernesses could be controls, "representative samples," that tell us how we are managing other areas. We know, though, that even in his early days in the Southwest Leopold was dabbling with some kind of Clements-like organicism. By the end of his life, he was urging a less utilitarian *land ethic*. The ethic affirmed the fundamental rights of soil, water, plants, and animals "to continued existence, and, at least in spots, their continued existence in a natural state."

Leopold died in 1948, at age sixty-one, just as he was working out the details of his land ethic. His death was connected, in a way, to his developing philosophy of land use. In the 1930s, Leopold had bought a ruined farm in central Wisconsin. He and his family drove to the land on weekends. They installed some bunks and a primitive kitchen in a chicken shed, the only building on the property. With what they called the "shack" as their base, they began to plant trees—some fifty thousand—and restore native plants to the farm. They hoped the trees would provide a backbone for the renewal of the land's disrupted ecological networks. Leopold, his wife, and one of their children were at the shack in 1948 when a fire on a neighbor's land threatened to undo the years of restoration. While helping the neighbor fight the fire, Leopold had a heart attack. He stretched out on the ground. By the time the fire front had swept over him and singed his skin, he was already dead.

At the time of his death, Leopold's major work on his land ethic was still unpublished. Many of his thoughts on the ethic had been developed for talks he gave while he was professor of wildlife management at the University of Wisconsin in the late 1930s and early 1940s. He had collected some of these talks, added a few more, assigned to the collection the title *Great Possessions*, and shipped it to two American trade book publishers. Both companies rejected it. Their editors complained that the essays in the collection lacked unity. The discouraged Leopold handed the manuscript over to his son Luna and turned his attention to other projects. Luna

The Oxford Press edition of Aldo Leopold's last book.

opened negotiations with Oxford University Press, and in mid-April of 1948 Oxford phoned to tell Aldo that it wanted to publish his essays.

Leopold and his family were ecstatic. But Oxford's timing was poor. A week after the phone call, Aldo Leopold lay dead on a Wisconsin road. The death of an author, unless the person has a major print following, usually means the cancellation of any unpublished books. Luna finessed the book through the publishing process, editing it with notes left behind by his father, keeping pressure on Oxford Press to honor its commitment. When the book appeared in 1949, retitled *A Sand County Almanac and Sketches Here and There*, it was well received—not so much by the public, perhaps, but certainly within the environmental circles where Leopold had spent much of his adult life. For the next twenty years the book continued to sell steadily, and by 1970 some twenty thousand copies were in print, a significant run for an author who was not around to promote his own book.

A thousand copies a year for twenty years is not bad, but not a best seller. Better times were ahead, though, for Leopold's posthumous book. The problem that bedeviled the book—the unity of its essays—was about to go away. Leopold himself believed that all the essays pointed in a single direction: they all spoke about an attitude that humans assumed, or ought to assume, toward the natural world. Leopold's awareness of environmental issues was not widely shared in the late 1940s. During the countercultural movement of the 1960s and 1970s, however, elements of this vision began to lodge themselves in a wider public. More readers were starting to understand what Leopold had been getting at in his little book. *A Sand County Almanac* was eventually adopted as a founding scripture of the new environmental movement, and sales took off. Millions of copies of the book were printed in nearly a dozen languages and today, six decades after it was first published, more copies are sold each day than were sold in a month during the 1950s.

I have looked in some detail at the fate of Leopold's little book because the changing reception of *A Sand County Almanac* marks a major expansion of Romantic nature-as-process during the second half of the twentieth century. During this step-five turn, Leopold's ideas about wilderness gained a political face, leading to the US Wilderness Act of 1964, which defined wilderness as an area "untrammeled by man, where man himself is a visitor who does not remain." The act was not, at the time of its passage, a tool to bring previously unprotected lands into the public domain. It was a meta-act, a way of layering a new conception of land preservation onto territories that already had some insulation from the mechanisms of the marketplace. Over the next five decades, large tracts of land, mostly properties controlled by the Forest Service and the Bureau of Land Management, were placed under the act's definitions. Eventually the wilderness system would come to embrace 5 percent of US lands, about a sixth of all lands in government hands. Thanks to the act, the term *wilderness*, already an important locus for the struggle between Enlightenment and Romantic ideas, moved to the forefront of the conflict between step-four and step-five views of nature.

The debate over wilderness—what it means, how to make it work in policy and practice—inevitably leads to a discussion of rights and intrinsic values, concepts that the Enlightenment tradition honed to a fine point in order to establish a humanistic framework for law and democratic government. The Romantic reaction adopted and adapted these humanitarian tools to argue for the parallel rights of nature. Many of the environmentalisms that emerged in the second half of the twentieth century—biocentrism, animal liberation, deep ecology—sought to assign intrinsic value to nonhuman organisms and systems. Their work has been encapsulated in the Earth Charter that has been endorsed by a large number of governments and international organizations. The charter states in its first point that "every form of life has value regardless of its worth to human beings." *A Sand County Almanac* has become an important text for these new movements because Leopold was one of the first writers to acknowledge the need for intrinsic natural value. In his essay "The Land Ethic," Leopold compares the struggle for natural rights to the struggle for human rights. Odysseus, he says, hanged on one rope a dozen slave girls from his household that he suspected of dalliance. There was no issue of their rights, only of his—they were his property and he could dispose of them at will. Our modern understanding of human rights finds his behavior reprehensible. "There is as yet," Leopold goes on to note, "no ethic dealing with man's relation to land and to the animals and plants which grow upon it. Land, like Odysseus' slave-girls, is still property." At some point, Leopold suggests, the status of nature will be lifted above low utilitarian goals that now motivate our land policies. Natural systems will gain an agency similar to the one we already recognize in people and their societies. When that happens, we will come to regard our current treatment of the earth and its natural systems with the same disgust that we now view Odysseus's slaughter of his human property.

෴

The transition to a Romantic, step-five view of nature is a paradigm shift. As I noted earlier, these shifts can make words behave in an odd way. Terms that were fully at home in an old paradigm can stretch and strain when borrowed by a new paradigm. Some of them never really settle in. We looked earlier at the problems caused by terms such as *race* and *species*. The word *wilderness* is another of these slippery terms.

Prior to the nineteenth century, Roderick Nash notes in *Wilderness and the American Mind*, wilderness "was instinctively understood as something alien, . . . as an obscure and uncomfortable environment against which civilization had waged an unceasing struggle." Europeans crossing the Atlantic wanted to reproduce the tame pastoral landscapes of the continent they had left behind. Landscapes that had not yet been given the European treatment were their wildernesses. For the Puritans, the unsettled North American wilderness was dark, mysterious, and threatening, the habitation of monsters and demons.

When Romantic ideas made their way across the same ocean in the first decades of the nineteenth century, the American wilderness began to take on a new look. Objectively, the word *wilderness* still referred to the same places: wilderness lands were those that had not been brought within the sphere of social utility. Subjectively, however, the word underwent a reversal. Wildernesses, once places of terror, became objects of affection and longing. Ralph Waldo Emerson, who launched the transcendental movement with his 1836 essay "Nature," advised his readers to put aside books and other trappings of civilization and turn toward natural settings for insight and inspiration: "In the wilderness, I find something more dear and connate than in streets or villages," he wrote. "In the tranquil landscape, and especially in the distant line of the horizon, man beholds somewhat as beautiful as his own nature." As the Romantic paradigm took hold, thinkers sought new ways to package the revised concept. The nineteenth century poets and artists who responded to the transcendentalist message began to celebrate something in natural settings that they called the *sublime*. The Wilderness Act of 1964 employed a number of creative synonyms for the wilderness lands designated by the act, phrases such as *primeval, primitive, natural condition,* and *affected primarily by the forces of nature*.

It was inevitable that thinkers would detect, sooner or later, some friction between the objective sense of the word *wilderness* and the new subjectivity that was being packed into it. The discussions, which go under the name *the new wilderness debate*, got started about 1990. Some five dozen of the hundreds of journal articles that make up the debate have been collected by J. Baird Callicott and Michael P. Nelson into two hefty volumes, *The Great New Wilderness Debate* and *The Wilderness Debate Rages On*.

The controversy, Callicott and Nelson note, got started when several journal articles called attention to the negative effects of the wilderness movement on tribal groups. A number of tribes had been or were about to be forced from their ancestral lands in order to make room for wilderness preserves. This initial issue gave rise to other criticisms of the wilderness movement, and for the next few years battles over the meaning of the word *wilderness* occupied ecologists and historians. The fight received wider attention in 1995, when William Cronon, winner of the Bancroft Prize, published "The Trouble with Wilderness" in the *New York Times Magazine* and in his book *Uncommon Ground*. The publicity generated by Cronon's piece brought other important thinkers into the debate, leading, says Callicott, to "name-calling, conference outbursts, accusations of strange bedfellows and political shape shifting, and even rumors of death threats."

At the heart of the debate, say the critics, is an impossible promise. The myth-eaten term *wilderness* barges into modern ecology from its home in our intuition and begins to attach itself to specific pieces of land, enchanting them with its Romantic associations. When this happens, say Callicott and Cronon, we set ourselves up for a major disappointment. No parcel of land can measure up to the standards set for it by a Romantic notion of wilderness. The tension between the ideal of wilderness and the gritty reality of lands actually designated as wilderness leads, these critics say, to three contradictions and paradoxes.

The journal articles that launched the new wilderness debate flagged the first of these contradictions. Preservation of wilderness lands has been a serious goal, the articles note, in only a limited number of countries. The movement has been strongest in North America, the United States in particular. Canada, though it has been less willing to embody the term wilderness in its statutes, retains at least as much of its land in a primitive state. Mexico has a smaller wilderness movement: less than 1 percent of the country has wilderness designation. Outside of North America, only the antipodal territories of the old British Empire—Australia, South Africa, and New Zealand—have significant wilderness movements. European countries tend to be sympathetic to the ecological ideals of the movements, but they have few large tracts of land in the public domain, and the ones that they do have usually fail North American tests for primitiveness.

When we get past this limited roster of countries, wilderness preservation encounters people problems. Candidate wilderness lands in South America, Asia, and Africa are often the home of aboriginals. If wilderness is characterized by the absence of humans and their artifacts, then people must be removed in order to turn these areas into wildernesses. Ramachandra Guha cites the tiger preserve at Nagarhole National Park in India's Karnataka State as an example. The park, which hosts about forty tigers, also has six thousand tribals "who have been in the area longer than anyone can remember, perhaps as long as the tigers themselves." The state's Forest Department, worried that the native people are taking game that the tigers need, wants the tribals to move. The Karnataka story is not an isolated one: almost every candidate wilderness on three continents, two-thirds of the world's land mass, faces the same issue. Even in locations where platting a wilderness reserve does not force local people to move, it can still deprive poor and indigenous peoples of crucial resources—places to scavenge fuel, places to hunt and gather food, places to graze animals, places to worship. Critics of the wilderness movement point the finger of hypocrisy at the lands in North America, Australia, and South Africa that are held up as wilderness models. Most of them only became people-free when indigenous groups were forced out of them or given only limited access to them. Victoria's Goldstream Park is a prime example.

A second contradiction exposed in the recent debate over wilderness concerns the standards used to designate lands as wilderness. In the early years of the campaign for wilderness lands, activists assumed that they could draw a bright line between developed and wilderness lands. In recent decades it has become clear that all wilderness lands have a certain artifice to them—that they are currently, or once have been, manipulated by humans.

William M. Denevan reviewed the pre-European occupation of North and South American lands in his 1992 article, "The Pristine Myth." Modern ideas of what undeveloped land should look like, Denevan notes, tend to be based on what European colonists saw during the 1700s. The colonists did not always realize that they were looking at the decadent remnants of an earlier human conquest. "By 1492," he writes, "Indian activity throughout the Americas had modified forest extent and composition, created and expanded grasslands, and rearranged microrelief via countless artificial earthworks. Agricultural fields were common, as were houses and towns and roads and trails." When Columbus arrived in the New World, North and South America hosted fifty to eighty million people living in what may have been a higher state of civilization than the European nations underwriting Columbus's voyages. All of this changed with mind-numbing speed. Over the next century and a half, the native populations would be reduced through disease and slaughter to a tenth of what they were. Their unmaintained lands, meanwhile, were invaded by the natural processes that the American aboriginals had once suppressed. The Romantics latched onto these gone-to-seed regions as examples of primeval forests. The American wilderness, in Francis Jennings's apt phrasing, was more like a widow than a virgin. Preserving lands as wilderness, Denevan concludes, does not mean holding them in the state that they were when the First Americans looked after them or in the state they were before any humans had settled North and South America. It means preserving them in the condition of declined management that the later waves of European settlers encountered.

Wilderness lands have not only been affected by past human occupation. They are also products of our current industrial civilization. A variety of anthropogenic effects invade lands now held in reserve. Most of the world's wilderness areas, for example, have lost their keystone predators. In the absence of keystone predators, prey species overtax the plant base and skew ecosystem operations. These areas are also challenged by invasive fauna and flora. Species carried in from half a world away occupy significant portions of most wilderness lands. Hawai'i may be the worst example of an invaded land: by one estimate, the majority of the terrestrial species in the Hawaiian Islands are postcolonial introductions. In addition to the altered flora and fauna, crafted chemicals creep into wilderness areas through the air and water. Nitrogen compounds, always important regulators of ecosystem function, fall onto and drain into the land from industrial sites hundreds of kilometers away. Excess phosphates, especially those produced by agribusiness, flow into remote areas via rain and river. Pesticides and heavy metals accumulate in wilderness food chains. Human activities also alter the macroclimates and microclimates on which many ecosystems depend. Land, we are learning, is not so different from the ocean. If we dump toxins into a body of water, they quickly diffuse through the fluid. What we do on land also spreads, through the agency of animals, insects, wind, and rain, to areas that are far removed from the point of pollution. Marla Cone describes in her book *Silent Snow* how DDT and PCBs hopscotch from their points of use in temperate North America, settle down in subarctic lands, and bioaccumulate up the food chains to menace the people and animals in nonindustrialized regions. What she calls *the Arctic paradox* causes Inuit in remote areas of Greenland to "carry more mercury and PCBs in their bodies than anyone else on earth."

The wilderness movement saddles us, finally, with a third contradiction. Defining wilderness in terms of human absence, says Baird Callicott, isolates humans from part of what they are. Humans become unnatural when human-empty areas become the prime expressions of nature. A millennium ago, even a few hundred years ago, we celebrated this unnaturalness, calling on the resources of theology and philosophy to draw a hard line between humans and nature. In our post-Darwin, post-Freud, process-infused world, this kind of line-drawing feels rigid. In addition, isolating nature from culture, as we do when we assign pristine examples of nature to segregated wilderness areas, gives us less reason to respect lands that fail the wilderness test. Since only a handful of the earth's people can make regular use of wilderness lands, the vast majority of us will gradually lose touch with nature. Unable to see the processes of nature at work in our daily context, we will stop recognizing these processes. Eventually we will stop valuing them.

∞

Threats to aboriginal cultures, confusions about what are and are not pristine natural states, the removal of humans from the natural realm— critics who are troubled by these contradictions between wilderness rhetoric and wilderness reality appeal, with some justification, to Aldo

Aldo Leopold in front of "the shack," a renovated chicken shed on a central Wisconsin farm. Image courtesy of the Aldo Leopold Foundation.

Leopold. We have looked so far at two segments of the arc of Leopold's life: Leopold as Forest Service manager and Leopold as a University of Wisconsin ecologist. In the first segment of his life, Leopold's understanding of nature and wilderness was largely utilitarian. He expanded the managerial perspective picked up from his teachers and colleagues by pressing for reserved lands, but he was still captive to a way of looking at nature that sectioned it into productive, human-useful parcels. In the second segment of his life, Leopold pursued an ecological vision that led him to attribute intrinsic value to natural systems. He helped found The Wilderness Society and called, in *A Sand County Almanac*, for "a militant minority of wilderness-minded citizens" to keep watch and be "vigilantly available for action" wherever there was an opportunity to preserve intact natural areas.

A two-segment take on Leopold's life doesn't, however, do justice to the full range of his interests. It divides his life by his attitudes toward wilderness, pretending that there was a sudden turn in his thinking that transformed his every idea into a before and an after. What we actually find in the arc of Leopold's life is a third segment that parallels the other two. Had Leopold lived another decade or two, we might have been able to assign the full expression of this segment to a specific stage of his life.

In this third segment, Leopold gives his attention, not to wilderness regions, but to conservation practices on privately owned land. The government's hand is always heavy in the quest for wilderness—only states can afford to quarantine large tracts of land and protect them from pressing economic needs. But relying too much on governments cuts across one of Leopold's deepest grains. In his heartwood, he was an individualist and a Jeffersonian democrat. His political attitudes were more comfortable with the policies of limited government that dominated the 1920s than with the statist policies of Franklin Roosevelt. Twice in his career Leopold unshackled himself from the bonds of government and university employment in order to work for private enterprise, once to do a year with the Albuquerque Chamber of Commerce, and again to carry out several years of game surveys for the Sporting Arms and Ammunition Manufacturer's Institute. When Roosevelt launched the Civilian Conservation Corps (CCC) in 1933, Leopold returned to the Southwest to supervise a summer section of the new CCC. The limited vision of CCC directors frustrated him. In an article he wrote the next year, Leopold described them as "brainy young technicians, many of them fresh from conservation schools, but each schooled only in his particular 'specialty.'" The crews they headed up often worked at cross-purposes. A road crew, for example, cut a grade across a clay bank and dumped sediment into a trout stream that another crew was trying to improve with dams and shelters. Leopold's CCC experiences underlined a belief he had acquired during his years in the Forest Service: trying to solve every social problem with a top-down solution was futile.

The issue of top-down conservation efforts came up again in the year following Leopold's stint in the CCC, when he was called in to advise the Soil Conservation Service on its first watershed project. Coon Valley, in Wisconsin's driftless area, was the site of devastating floods in the 1920s. The European settlers who had moved into the valley in the previous century had farmed it in ways that increased erosion. Coon Valley had become, Leopold wrote, "one of the thousand farm communities which, through the abuse of its originally rich soil, has not only filled the national dinner pail, but has created the Mississippi flood problem, the navigation problem, the overproduction problem, and the problem of its own future continuity." He helped the Soil Conservation Service provide planning and incentives for local landowners, and the reforms that were adopted by sympathetic farmers spread to their neighbors. At the end of the project, the various innovations championed by Leopold—contour plowing, steep slopes fenced off from cattle, erosion control, crop rotation—became standard practices in the region. The floods of the 1920s did not return. Leopold was impressed by the way government had allowed individual Coon Valley landowners to take initiative. "It is easy to side-step the issue of getting lumbermen to practice forestry, or the farmer to crop game or conserve soil," he wrote, "and pass these functions to government. *But it won't work.*" The great need, he says, is to "induce the private landowner to conserve on his own land." Leopold's vision of a land ethic, often understood by his later readers in the context of his work on state-initiated wilderness preservation, was primarily directed at sustainable practices on less-than-pristine private land. It is this side of Leopold, this underrecognized segment of his life, that appeals to the recent critics of the wilderness idea. "Leopold envisioned throughout his life," says Baird Callicott, "an ideal of human unity and harmony with nature, rather than a trade-off between human economic activities and environmental quality."

In the first part of his professional life, Leopold adopted Theodore Roosevelt as a hero and model. The young forester labored to advance the goals of the Forest Service, an institution that Roosevelt had founded. Leopold treasured throughout his life a short note of congratulations that he had received from the ex-president in 1917, two years before Roosevelt died. In the second segment of Leopold's life, Henry David Thoreau replaced Roosevelt. *A Sand County Almanac*, its many readers have noted, echoes Thoreau's *Walden* in style and outlook. We have no hero for the last, brief part of Leopold's life. Had he lived longer, he might have taken inspiration from the experiences of a sixteenth-century Dominican friar, Bartolomé de Las Casas.

De Las Casas was one of the first Europeans to take the side of the Indians against their Spanish overlords. He argued in his writings that the *encomienda* system, by which the Spanish crown parceled out to several thousand families the right to commandeer the work of the Indians, was a moral travesty. *Encomenderos* were slaughtering and working to death millions of Indians. Many of the friars and priests who were active in the New World supported de Las Casas's position. He captured the ear of the Spanish royal family, and the king backstopped several of de Las Casas's proposed reforms with royal law. But the work of a king and a few clerics on behalf of the suffering Indians could not turn the tide. The New World settlers refused to obey laws that would compel them to give up their control of indigenous forced labor. Spain, needing money for its European intrigues, delayed decisive action on the recalcitrant *encomenderos*. Not until the native populations had been reduced to a level where they were no longer worth exploiting would Spain's damaging New World policies be reversed. Greed and ambition, de Las Casas lamented at the end of his life, "have destroyed the Indies."

The experience of de Las Casas underlines a persistent problem with morally good ideas. Progressive ideals that are couched as rational arguments seldom reach, even when they are widely disseminated, more than a small fraction of the population. Unless this fraction has extraordinary access to sources of power and money, their efforts will fail. Social momentum almost always trumps good ideas—a maxim we might call *the de Las Casas principle*.

Leopold understood the de Las Casas principle in his bones. He believed that only the diffusion of a populist land ethic, an unwritten moral code that made itself felt in cities and farms as well as in wilderness, could make an abiding difference. When critics of the wilderness idea complain that the wilderness movement relies too much on the moral indignation of a vocal minority undergirded by government sponsorship, they stand with Leopold. They find, in the third segment of Leopold's career, a third view of wilderness: not a threatening, waiting-to-be-tamed wild, not a sublime presence in untouched lands, but an agent that negotiates with human society a common, complex future.

∾

At the beginning of the twenty-first century, we find ourselves in a conceptual boundary layer, sandwiched between the older Enlightenment perspectives on nature—step four in our progression—and the more recent Romantic views. Boundary layers, as we have seen in this book, develop their own set of rules. When viewed from the more stable spheres that give rise to the boundary, these rules can seem confused. Inside the boundary layer, however, the rules come to have plain, widely accepted interpretations.

The new perspectives birthed inside a conceptual boundary layer often give us new meanings for words. The term *sustainable*, which is popular with the critics in the new wilderness debate—Cronon, Callicott, and others—is one of these changed words. Outside the boundary layer occupied by these critics, in the regions dominated by Romantic and Enlightenment absolutes, the word doesn't have good traction. A sustainable practice for the Enlightenment-inspired industrialist is one that achieves a maximum rate of extraction without triggering environmental costs that interfere with business. Unsustainable actions, from this point of view, are few and far between. To the Romantic, in contrast, almost no human activity is sustainable. Everything we do inside of reserved wildernesses nudges them in human directions. Those standing within the boundary layer, in contrast, are not forced into these all-or-nothing takes. The rules in the borderlands allow those who live there to use the terms *sustainable* and *unsustainable* in new ways.

The word *wilderness* also takes on a fresh meaning in the boundary layer. If the critics in the new wilderness debate have their way, the term will shed its Romantic association with strict hands-off preservation. The lands that we have become accustomed to labeling as wildernesses, says Emma Marris in *Rambunctious Garden*, will "become anchors, with overlapping zones of various protection regimes and conservation goals radiating out from them, like petals from the center of a rose." As we begin to look at the wild in a different way, new public attitudes toward nature may emerge, leading us at last to something like Leopold's elusive land ethic.

We might also hope that the perspective emerging in this boundary layer will give us advice about Goldstream Park. The Enlightenment tradition tried to bring the park within its sphere by hooking into its minerals, its energy resources, and its tourism potential. When the land was turned into a park, it moved into the Romantic sphere. Goldstream is not a place, however, that conforms to Romantic measures of wilderness. Too many parties—the transportation industry that needs its highway corridor, the First Nation tribes and sportfishers that take its salmon, the recreation contingent that maintains its overused trails and campgrounds—crowd to the table when questions about land use arise. To manage Goldstream and the thousands of other wild nature reserves that live close to human-altered landscapes, we must move outside Enlightenment and Romantic perspectives and into the layer between them.

Luck—or miracle—gave us Goldstream Park. Perhaps the evolution of a conceptual boundary layer will tell us what we should do with it.

I was searching for something a little more than a dashing metaphor,
a good deal less than a cultural map.
— C. P. Snow, *The Two Cultures*

ॐ

Epilogue

On these visits to British Columbia's living laboratory, I've tapped into the vocabulary of the sciences. It's how I've learned to think about the denizens of the stegnon. Here and there, though, fragments of another vocabulary have risen to the surface, reminding me that my search for one kind of boundary layer has taken place within another kind of boundary layer—the one inside the borderlands between the sciences, where I've spent half of my educational and professional life, and the humanities, which have occupied the other half.

In the middle years of the twentieth century, the British physicist/novelist/politician C. P. Snow complained about the abrupt boundary between the sciences and the humanities. Those who work in the two fields, said Snow, belong to two separate cultures that view each other across a "gulf of mutual incomprehension." Their attitudes are "so different that, even on the level of emotion, they can't find much common ground." The situation has not improved in recent decades. It may, in fact, have gotten worse. The sciences and the humanities, to judge by my own experience, don't like to talk to each other even when they are stuffed into a single head.

The feud in my head has been handled, for the most part, by letting the two sides go their own ways. The sciences and the humanities prefer, like the positive and negative poles of a battery, the insulation of distance. Once in a while, though, the two sides wander too close to each other. When that happens, a spark leaps between the poles, and I get a glimpse of some larger universe in which the two sides of myself inhabit, for a brief moment, the same head.

The sparks have been infrequent, but memorable. The first of these sparks fired during the late years of my adolescence. In my teens, I was a science geek. I became aware as I got older, however, that there were other ways of looking at the world than through the eyes of science. These alternate views were more at home in humanities subjects. I decided to abandon my intellectual home and set out on a voyage through the humanities.

This long-ago switch from the sciences to the humanities comes to me now as a mash of disconnected memories. In one of these internal videos, I am sitting in a rocking chair in my upstairs room in a prairie ranch house, pushing back and forth, a philosophy text with an orange-brown cover opened on my lap. The sun has just set, and the mourning doves that nest outside my windows have taken up their evening cooing. I'm thinking about what I have read, and it suddenly occurs to me that the ideas that excite philosophers are for the most part two-party competitions. Universal versus particular is one of the oldest of these contested dichotomies. There are also philosophical debates around necessity versus free will, subject versus object, rule-based versus utilitarian morality, and rational versus empirical knowledge. Science, I knew, also had its dichotomies: nature-nurture, catastrophism-uniformitarianism, quantum-classical, and so on. I wondered if there might be one of these divisions, taken from either the sciences or the humanities, that could house all of the others. I didn't know which one it was, but I thought that, if I ranged broadly enough in my study and reading, I might one day find it.

The memory of this early vision of unity faded with the years. I didn't lose all sight of what I had glimpsed that evening, though. It was probably the reason that I found myself, some ten years later, in a graduate philosophy program at the University of Chicago. The philosophy department at the university was dominated in those days by a school of thought known as analytic philosophy. Thinkers in this school were skilled at handling the abstractions I had glimpsed when I was eighteen. My teachers spent much of their time exploring the classical dichotomies of philosophy, teasing out their strengths and weaknesses. We talked in our classes about category mistakes, conceptual clarity, and language games. After spending some years working with analytic methods, I began to wonder whether the toolkit I was acquiring would ever lead to tangible results. Studying philosophy of science from the analytic perspective, I remember, was particularly disappointing—instead of connecting philosophy to the sciences, it made the social and intellectual chasm between the sciences and the humanities feel even wider.

It was during one of these bouts of doubt that I signed up for a course on the philosopher Hegel. I didn't know much about Hegel at the time, but I was aware that he had tried to deal with some of the same issues that were troubling me. In the first weeks of the class, I struggled to understand Hegel's texts. His writings presented me with some of the densest philosophical code I had ever encountered. After banging my head against his sentences for two months, I began to get the hang of his system. My long-standing problem with the separation between the sciences and the humanities, I started to realize, was due—in part at least—to attitudes that I had brought to the issue. I had assumed that comprehensive knowledge could only be found at the end of a process of increasing abstraction. We needed, I thought, to look at the world from ever higher standpoints that gave wider panoramas of the intellectual landscape. Hegel handled these climbs in a different way. He ascended the hills of abstraction only far enough to see how abstract contradictions created a middle ground between them. He would then walk down the hill and immerse himself in the middle ground that was the living truth of the two extremes.

I couldn't buy into the whole system Hegel offered—few moderns can. His dialectical methods, though, gave me a new way to approach the conflict between the sciences and the humanities. He turned me away from a quest for abstraction and toward a concrete and dynamic sociology of knowledge. By the time I emerged from my tutelage with Hegel, I knew that a spark had leaped between my twin interests. The light of that second spark, as it turned out, illuminated a bridge to an earlier interest in the sciences, one I had set aside to study philosophy. After a few more years in philosophy and humanities, I crossed that bridge and took up residence in the land of science.

When I started writing the pieces that make up this book, looking at how stable paired natural systems gave rise to regions between them and how these border regions demanded to be understood in their own terms, it dawned on me that I was meeting up with old friends. These boundary regions were examples of Hegel's synthetic middles. They were generated by the clash of large, self-contained systems, and they took advantage of this clash to come up with their own practical rules.

This similarity between the dynamics of a science metaphor and some half-remembered metaphysics from an earlier academic life occurred to me about halfway through the interviews that led to this book. The insight sat there, not really leading anywhere, until I reached the final chapter. When I started looking at the boundary layer between nature and society, a question—an absurdly simple question—popped into my head.

I had lifted a metaphor out of Prandtl's exploration of boundary layers in moving fluids. When we create metaphors, they latch on to a relation in one field and transpose it into another. I had taken Prandtl's insight into the physical boundary layer between fluids and nonfluids and applied it, while writing the chapters of this book, to topics in biology. As an example, take the section on mycorrhizal mushrooms: mycorrhizas live in a boundary layer between two large systems, the world of plants and the world of fungi. A diagram of the metaphor at work in the section on mycorrhizas might look like this:

The metaphorical move.

The big arrow is the metaphorical move. The relation on the left is the literal grounding, the one on the right is the resulting metaphor.

Throughout this book Prandtl's boundary layer has served as the left-hand, literal sense of my metaphors about mushrooms, lichens, mosses, ecosystems, and nature.

What does it mean, though, to say that Prandtl's boundary layer is the literal side of the metaphor? When Prandtl used the phrase *boundary layer*, the term was already a metaphor. It had its grounding in some other field and Prandtl borrowed what it meant in that field in order to discuss mechanics of fluids. What, I wondered, was the source, the literal ground, of his own metaphor?

Prandtl himself was silent about the underpinnings of his image. When we look at the 1904 essay that launched the metaphor, however, we see that Prandtl uses the German word *Grenzschicht*, later translated as boundary layer, only once. His term of preference is *Übergangsschicht*, which is often rendered into English as *transition layer*. This translation, however, falls short of the range of meaning packed into the German term. *Übergangsschicht* lays more stress on the movement that leads to the transition. Prandtl's preferred term for his boundary regions is, if you like, *the going-over layer*. This term, *going over* (*Übergang*), occurs frequently in Hegel's philosophy and in later German idealism. It was a buzzword that expressed the Romantic sense of dynamic process, calling attention to the way that conflicting abstractions do not remain static, but transform themselves into living middles. Prandtl was not a philosopher, of course, and he would not have employed the coded term with metaphysical precision. But the word and the concept were in the air in late nineteenth-century Germany, and Prandtl would have acquired them—along with their metaphysics—as easily as he breathed.

When we explore the boundary layers in natural systems, then, we look back not only *to* Prandtl and his moving fluids, but also *through* Prandtl to the more fundamental understanding of thought and spirit that set the context for his work. Behind the dry mathematics of Prandtl's science we catch a glimpse of a Romantic quest for process that had come to dominate work in the humanities. His boundary layer metaphor, the one on which I lean so heavily in this book, turns out to be an early fusion of the vocabularies of the sciences and the humanities.

My glimpse of this earlier fusion made me wonder: Could my attraction to boundary layers in natural systems be an unconscious expression of the sciences-humanities rift I have carried inside me? Science-based ecologists do not usually own up to their debt to the vocabulary of the humanities, any more than the mathematician Prandtl confesses to his borrowings from Romantic philosophy, but those of us with tents in both camps tend to notice the words that sneak back and forth at night. Aldo Leopold had one of these double minds. As his daughter Nina points out, he often found himself straddling the divide that C. P. Snow would later attribute to separate cultures. On a visit to ecological sites in prewar Germany, Leopold jotted these sentences on a piece of hotel stationery: "One of the anomalies of modern ecology is that it is the creation of two groups, each of which seems barely aware of the existence of the other. The one studies the human community almost as if it were a separate entity, and calls its findings sociology, economics, and history. The other studies the plant and animal community and comfortably relegates the hodge-podge of politics to the 'liberal art.'" He goes on to predict "the inevitable fusion of these two lines of thought."

As I wrap up this story of boundary layers and natural systems, I realize that the spark has jumped again. Not, this time, with the emotional voltage it had in my adolescence, and not with the intellectual amperage of my middle years. It comes instead as a rising surge that closes, for a moment, some of the open circuits in my mind.

The tension between science and the humanities is my own deepest rift. It is the question I bring to the practical genius in the boundary layer. The polarizations that take up residence in our culture are legion, however, and others will no doubt carry their own concerns to and from the oracle in the boundary layer. Some of these rifts may be conceptual ones. In this book I have touched on a few of these—whether ecosystems exist and have rights, where we draw the lines that separate wilderness from civilization. Some may find themselves racked by the more tangible dichotomies embedded in our research paradigms. We have seen a few of the problems that these dichotomies introduce into the study of the mosses, lichens, fungi, and plants in the overlooked stegnon. All of these divisions, whether abstract or concrete, give rise to their own boundary layers, and boundary layers, as we have seen, become birthing grounds for new rules, rules that can change the way we look at both nature and human nature.

Acknowledgments

This book started out *in ovo* some fifteen years ago, while I was still living in central Canada. *Queen's Quarterly*, a literary journal based in Kingston, Ontario, published an article of mine with the title "Boundary Layer." In the essay, I narrated my explorations of the biotic life just above and below the soil line. The article's name was a play on words. *Boundary layer*, as this book explains, is a technical term for a transition zone. To muck about in the atmospheric boundary layer, I had to lay myself down in this narrow region, to get face to face with the soil.

When I moved to the Pacific Northwest nine years ago, I found myself drawn once again to the overlooked biological zones along the ground. The boundary layers in British Columbia, however, were quite different from the ones I had known in the East. Here the mosses, fungi, lichens, and small plants of the boundary layers were more bold, more lush. They had a commanding presence in their ecological networks. Intrigued by this new environment, I wrote several articles about the denizens of this lower region for Pacific Northwest magazines. I also started giving talks to natural history organizations and taking groups on guided walks. In 2008, when I finished the social history volume that had occupied me for several years, I decided it was time to get book-serious about the boundary layer.

These essays owe a great debt to the army of biologists who spend their lives investigating the inhabitants of the stegnon. Without them, all would be speculation. But the solemnities of their science did not always satisfy my stegnon questions. Vocabularies sharpened on macroflora and macrofauna have a tendency to carve away the most interesting issues posed by borderland organisms. Some of these less-than-orthodox questions, I found, were already being asked by those immersed in detailed research on stegnon organisms. Bringing the lives and words of these inquisitive people into the text became a way to explore such questions. Danielle Bellefleur, Oluna and Adolf Ceska, Darren and Claudia Copley, Trevor Goward, Terry McIntosh, Andy MacKinnon, Andrea Pickart, Hans Roemer, and Carl Sieber generously donated their time to help me learn not only what they knew about the borderlands, but also what they didn't know. My profound thanks to them for letting their speculative thoughts appear in print. Since books take time to write (three years for this book) and the lag between publication and reading can be long, I provide updates about the current activities of these eleven helpers on the book's web site, stegnon.com. You will also find on this site additional materials related to the book.

To other Pacific Northwest naturalists who do not appear in these pages by name, my thanks for hours of profitable walks and talks. Gerry, Agnes, Deb, Moralea, Sinclair, Ian, Matt, and Wynne were there for me when I needed to know more. Professionals from several fields provided feedback on specific chapters: my thanks to Ernie Brodo, Bernard Goffinet, Ian Walker, and Jan Drabek for reviewing chapter drafts. They bear no responsibility for my slant on the material, of course. Will MacKenzie helped me chase down an image. Thanks also to Erin, Jeanne, Mim, and David, who read and corrected complete versions of this text, and to my kin network in our British Columbia family compound for their support. Mary Elizabeth Braun and the staff at Oregon State University Press deserve (and get) my sincere thanks for their patience and persistence over the months and years it has taken to put this book in front of the reading public. Susan Campbell lent her editing expertise to prepare the book for print.

Parts of this book have appeared, in altered form, in *Fungi* magazine, *BC Nature*, and *Victoria Naturalist*. The image on the cover was painted by Joanne Thomson (joannethomson.com). Joanne was artist in residence at Capital Regional District Parks when I did a moss walk/talk, and the watercolor study was her interpretation of a moss we saw that day, tree moss (*Leucolepis acanthoneura*).

Sources

vii   *there is no such thing on earth as an uninteresting subject.* G. K. Chesterton, *Heretics* (Rockville, Maryland: Serenity Publishers, 2009), 23.

xi   *stegnon.* Definition from Trevor Goward, email message to author, July 20, 2012.

xi   *we might choose 1862.* In a study of the relationship between epidemics and First Nations populations, Robert Boyd makes the following connections between disease and the loss of Native majorities: "the 'fever and ague' [probably malaria] in western Oregon after 1830, with Indian depopulation and a White majority by 1845; 1848 measles and 1853 smallpox in western Washington, with indigenous depopulation and a White majority by 1858; and 1862 smallpox and depopulation in Native coastal British Columbia and a White majority by the early 1880s." Robert Boyd, *The Coming of the Spirit of Pestilence: Introduced Infectious Diseases and Population Decline among Northwest Coast Indians, 1774–1874* (Vancouver: UBC Press, 1999), 4. In 1958, to mark the one-hundredth anniversary of the commencement of the Western Canada gold rush that led to British Columbia's 1871 entry into the confederation, Canada minted a gold coin. Ironically, the *death dollar,* as it came to be called, had a totem pole on the reverse side that prominently featured a raven, for certain tribes a symbol of death.

1   *do thou the substance of my matter see.* John Bunyan, "The Conclusion," *The Pilgrim's Progress,* ed. Susan L. Rattiner (Mineola, New York: Dover Publications, 2003), 168.

3   *Prandtl gave the world the earliest mathematical description of a* Grenzschicht. L. Prandtl, "Über Flüssigkeitsbewegung bei sehr kleiner Reibung," *Verhandlungen des Dritten Internationalen Mathematiker-Kongresses in Heidelberg vom 8. bis 13. August 1904,* ed. A. Krazer (Leipzig: B. G. Teubner, 1905), 484–491.

12   *a woodsman living along an isolated stretch of the West Coast Trail.* Ecologist Matt Fairbarns has taken the lead in documenting the story of pink sand-verbena. See Parks Canada, *Recovery Strategy for the Pink Sand-verbena* (Abronia umbellata) *in Canada,* by M. D. Fairbarns et al., Species at Risk Act Recovery Strategy Series (Ottawa: Parks Canada Agency).

21   *may be feasible over small areas for specific purposes.* Alfred M. Wiedemann and
     Andrea Pickart, "The *Ammophila* Problem on the Northwest Coast of
     North America," *Landscape and Urban Planning* 34 (1996): 291–292.

25   *travel and society polish one.* This line occurs in Burrough's handwritten jour-
     nal in the heading for November 18, 1877. The page can be viewed on
     a Vassar Archives site: http://digitallibrary.vassar.edu/islandora/object/
     vassar:19777#page/71/mode/1up (accessed October 30, 2015)

27   *one finds among the world's most sophisticated people.* Annie Dillard, *For the Time
     Being* (New York: Viking Press, 1999), 162.

28   *vascular plants get an unfair share of academic attention.* A documented plea to
     redress this balance can be found in Ricardo Rozzi, Juan J. Armesto, Ber-
     nard Goffinet, et al., "Changing Lenses to Assess Biodiversity: Patterns
     of Species Richness in Sub-Antarctic Plants and Implications for Global
     Conservation," *Frontiers in the Ecology and the Environment* 6 (2007): 131–137.
     The invertebrate/vertebrate ratio is mentioned in J. Alan Clark and Robert
     M. May, "Taxonomic Bias in Conservation Research," *Science* 297 (12 July
     2002): 191–192.

27   *what some researchers have begun to call the* bryosphere. Zoë Lindo and Andrew
     Gonzalez, "The Bryosphere: An Integral and Influential Component of
     the Earth's Biosphere," *Ecosystems* 13 (June 2010): 612–627.

28   *the most widespread plant.* Ron Porley and Nick Hodgetts, *Mosses and Liverworts*
     (London: Collins, 2001), 78.

33   *the volume on antarctic mosses that came out in 2008.* Ryszard Ochyra et al., *Il-
     lustrated Moss Flora of Antarctica* (Cambridge: Cambridge University Press,
     2008).

37   *research carried out by Nalini Nadkarni and her associates.* See, for example, Nalini
     M. Nadkarni, "Epiphyte Biomass and Nutrient Capital of a Neotropical
     Elfin Forest," *Biotropica* 16 (1984): 249–256.

43   *mushrooms in brine.* Alexander Pushkin, *Eugene Onegin*, tr. Charles Johnston
     (London: Penguin, 1977), chapter 2, stanza 32.

46   *fungi expand the surface area of some root systems sixty-fold.* Suzanne Simard et
     al., "Carbon and Nutrient Fluxes within and between Mycorrhizal Plants,"
     Mycorrhizal Ecology 157 (2002): 33–74. Cited in Nancy C. Johnson and
     Catherine A. Gehring, "Mycorrhizas: Symbiotic Mediators of Rhizo-
     sphere and Ecosystem Processes," *The Rhizosphere: An Ecological Perspective*,
     ed. Z. G. Cardon and J. L. Whitbeck (Amsterdam: Academic Press, 2007),
     78.

46   *soil ecologists have discovered that springtails.* John N. Klironomos and Miranda M. Hart, "Food-Web Dynamics: Animal Nitrogen Swap for Plant Carbon," *Nature* 410 (5 April 2001): 651–652.

50   *what does that* mean? Donella Meadows, "The Forest Is More Than a Collection of Trees," July 8, 1999, http://www.donellameadows.org/archives/the-forest-is-more-than-a-collection-of-trees/ (accessed February 1, 2013).

50   *coded in the* woodwide web. The term was apparently coined by an editor of *Nature* for the cover of the magazine's August 7, 1997 issue. The source of the phrase is described in Susan Goldhor, "The Woodwide Web or Capitalism and Socialism in the Forest," *Fungi* 6 (Fall 2013): 43.

53   *Oluna's surveys of Observatory Hill have turned up more than a thousand different species.* By the end of the 2012–2013 season, Oluna Ceska had found more than eleven hundred species. Archived yearly reports are indexed and linked on E-Flora BC, http://www.geog.ubc.ca/biodiversity/eflora/macro-fungi_observatory_hill.html (accessed October 30, 2015).

58   *Braun-Blanquet's 1928* Pflanzensoziologie. Josias Braun-Blanquet, *Pflanzensoziologie: Grundzüge der Vegetationskunde*, 3rd edition (Vienna: Springer Verlag, 1964). The English translation of the first edition is Josias Braun-Blanquet, *Plant Sociology: The Study of Plant Communities*, trans. and ed. George D. Fuller and Henry S. Conard (New York: Stechert-Hafner Service Agency, 1932).

59   *the first book-length biography appeared.* Jan Drabek, *Vladimir Krajina: World War II Hero and Ecology Pioneer* (Vancouver, British Columbia: Ronsdale Press, 2012).

65   *we can never know how wide a circle of disturbance.* George Perkins Marsh, *The Earth as Modified by Human Action* (New York: Scribner, Armstrong & Company, 1874), 144.

65   *can be seen on the Internet.* https://www.for.gov.bc.ca/hre/becweb/program/history/ (accessed October 30, 2015)

69   *1986 survey of members of the British Ecological Society.* A report of the preliminary results of the survey can be found in Malcolm Cherrett, "Ecological Concepts—the Results of the Survey of British Ecological Society Members' Views," *Bulletin of the Ecological Society of America* 70 (March 1989): 41–42.

69   *a community of organisms and its environment.* Definition from online Merriam-Webster Dictionary, http://www.merriam-webster.com/dictionary/ecosystem (accessed February 4, 2013).

70   *it is a commonplace truth.* "S'il est une vérité banale aujourd'hui, c'est que les langues sont des organismes vivants dont la vie . . . n'en est pas moins

réelle et peut se comparer à celle des organismes du règne végétal ou du règne animal." Arsène Darmesteter, *La Vie des Mots*, 3rd edition (Paris: Librairie Ch. Delagrave, 1889), 3.

72   *escaped professor.* Edith S. Clements, *Adventures in Ecology: Half a Million Miles . . . from Mud to Macadam* (New York: Pageant Press, 1956), 102.

72   *Clements coauthored with his friend Shelford a book.* Frederic E. Clements and Victor E. Shelford, *Bio-Ecology* (New York: John Wiley & Sons, 1939).

73   *climax formation is an organic entity.* Frederic E. Clements, *Plant Succession and Indicators* (New York: H. W. Wilson, 1916), 2.

73   *a unified mechanism in which the whole is greater than the sum of its parts.* Frederic E. Clements, *Dynamics of Vegetation*, ed. B. W. Allred and Edith S. Clements (New York: H. W. Wilson, 1949), 1.

73   *the fortuitous juxtaposition of plants.* H. A. Gleason, "Delving into the History of American Ecology," *Bulletin of the Ecological Society of America* 56 (December 1975): 10.

74   *in an early chapter of his 1939* Bio-Ecology. In chapter 2 of Frederic E. Clements and Victor E. Shelford, *Bio-Ecology* (New York: John Wiley & Sons, 1939), 21–24.

74   *a complex organism, or superorganism.* Frederic E. Clements and Victor E. Shelford, *Bio-Ecology* (New York: John Wiley & Sons, 1939), 20.

74   *species do not fit naturally into groupings.* Robert H. Whittaker, "Approaches to Classifying Vegetation," *Ordination and Classification of Communities*, ed. Robert H. Whittaker (The Hague: Dr. W. Junk, 1973), 327.

75   *a temporary gathering of strangers.* The wording used to describe Gleason's perspective by Donald Worster, *The Wealth of Nature: Environmental History and the Ecological Imagination* (Oxford: Oxford University Press, 1993), 163.

76   *interacting and connected biotic and abiotic components.* S. E. Jørgensen, "Introduction," *Ecosystem Ecology*, ed. Sven Erik Jørgensen (Amsterdam: Elsevier, 2009), 3.

76   *no redeeming vices.* Pound's comment is cited in Joel B. Hagen, "Clementsian Ecologists: The Internal Dynamics of a Research School," *Osiris*, 2nd Series 9 (1993): 182. Hagen says the quotation is taken from an Edith Clements manuscript, "Biography of Frederic E. Clements," 2, that is in Box 109 of the Frederic E. Clements Collection, University of Wyoming.

77   *almost 13 percent of the earth's land area has been set aside.* United Nations Environment Programme World Conservation Monitoring Centre (UNEP-WCMC), "Protected Planet Report 2012," 2012, http://cmsdata.iucn.org/downloads/protected_planet_report.pdf (accessed January 24, 2013). The

current reserve represents an almost 50 percent increase since 1990. The report tracks progress toward the Convention on Biological Diversity's goal to manage and conserve 17 percent of the world's terrestrial area by 2020.

77   *how ecosystems are distributed through their territories.* Roger L. Disilvestro, *Reclaiming the Last Wild Places: A New Agenda for Biodiversity* (New York: John Wiley & Sons, 1993), 203–204, uses calculations done by Reed Noss to show just how unbalanced wilderness protection programs are with respect to ecosystem variety. Of the 261 ecosystems recognized in the United States and Puerto Rico in the early 1990s, only five ecosystems were represented by wilderness reserves larger than a million hectares, a size sometimes cited as self-sustaining. Only fifty ecosystem types had wilderness reserves above a hundred thousand hectares.

77   *habitats with important ecological functions.* United Nations, Secretariat of the Convention on Biological Diversity, *The Convention on Biological Diversity Plant Conservation Report: A Review of Progress in Implementing the Global Strategy of Plant Conservation (GSPC)* (2009), 18.

81   *conserving and managing representative examples.* British Columbia, BC Parks, "BC Parks Conservation Program," http://www.env.gov.bc.ca/bcparks/conserve/cpp_p1/conserve.pdf (accessed February 4, 2013).

89   *a house is the shape which a man's thoughts.* Henry Ward Beecher, *Star Papers* (New York: J. C. Derby, 1855), 285.

93   *built on Humboldt's . . . work to found the science of statistics.* Laura Dassow Walls, *The Passage to Cosmos: Alexander von Humboldt and the Shaping of America* (Chicago: The University of Chicago Press, 2009), 109.

93   *the greatest scientific traveler who ever lived.* Charles Darwin, letter to J. D. Hooker, August 6, 1881, in *Life and Letters of Charles Darwin* , vol. 2, ed. Francis Darwin (New York: D. Appleton and Company, 1891), 422.

94   *the connection of facts . . . to the knowledge of insulated facts.* Alexander von Humboldt, *Personal Narrative of Travels to the Equinoctial Regions of the New Continent during the Years 1799–1804*, vol. 1, trans. Helen Maria Wilson (London: Longman, Hurst, Rees, Orme and Brown, 1822–1829), iv.

97   *remnants of old virus genes.* Sam Kean, in *The Violinist's Thumb* (New York: Little, Brown and Company, 2012), 143, mentions that "8 percent of our genome isn't human at all: a quarter billion of our base pairs are old virus genes."

97   *a summation of the genes embedded in our own human genome.* Jeffrey I. Gordon, "The Gordon Lab," http://gordonlab.wustl.edu (accessed January 29, 2013).

98   *questions about the human microbiome are new.* Peter J. Turnbaugh et al., "The Human Microbiome Project," *Nature* 449 (October 2007): 804.

98   *"emerging frontier" of insect symbioses.* Eric J. Caldera et al., "Insect Symbioses: A Case Study of Past, Present, and Future Fungus-growing Ant Research," *Environmental Entomology* 38 (2009): 79.

98   *one ant is . . . a vast disappointment.* Bert Hölldobler and E. O. Wilson, *The Leafcutter Ants: Civilization by Instinct* (New York: W. W. Norton & Company, 2011), 8.

99   *exists at a level of biological organization.* Bert Hölldobler and E. O. Wilson, *The Superorganism* (New York: W. W. Norton & Company, 2008), *xviii.*

98   *"operational" units with "emergent traits"* Bert Hölldobler and E. O. Wilson, *The Superorganism* (New York: W. W. Norton, 2008), 10.

99   *they make up the bulk of the animal biomass in some ecosystems.* Bert Hölldobler and E. O. Wilson, *The Superorganism* (New York: W. W. Norton, 2008), 4–5.

99   *the colony is the unit that we must examine.* Bert Hölldobler and E. O. Wilson, *The Leafcutter Ants: Civilization by Instinct* (New York: W. W. Norton & Company, 2011), 8.

100   *author of a classroom text on botanical microscopy.* Carl Nägeli and Simon Schwendener, *Das Mikroskop: Theorie und Anwendung desselben* (Leipzig: Wilhelm Engelmann, 1867).

103   *Readings on the Lichen Thallus.* The Ways of Enlichenment, http://www.waysofenlichenment.net/ (accessed February 4, 2012).

104   *I no longer see the world.* Trevor Goward, "Face in the Mirror," "Readings on the Lichen Thallus," The Ways of Enlichenment, http://www.waysofenlichenment.net/essays/readings_1_face.pdf (accessed February 4, 2012).

104   *names given to lichens apply to their fungal component.* International Code of Nomenclature for Algae, Fungi, and Plants (Melbourne Code), Art. 13.1(d), International Association for Plant Taxonomy, http://www.iapt-taxon.org/nomen/main.php?page=art13 (accessed February 4, 2012).

105   *grow in coordinated fashion.* Trevor Goward, "Re-emergence," "Readings on the Lichen Thallus," The Ways of Enlichenment, http://www.waysofenlichenment.net/essays/readings_4_reemergence.pdf (accessed February 4, 2012).

105   *a level of physiological integration and sophistication.* Trevor Goward, "Credo," "Readings on the Lichen Thallus," The Ways of Enlichenment, http://www.waysofenlichenment.net/essays/readings_3_credo.pdf (accessed February 4, 2012).

105 *some of lichenology's most basic questions.* Trevor Goward, "Conversational," "Readings on the Lichen Thallus," The Ways of Enlichenment, http://www.waysofenlichenment.net/essays/readings_5_conversational.pdf (accessed February 4, 2012).

113 *only that which has no history is definable.* "Alle Begriffe, in denen sich ein ganzer Prozess . . . zusammenfasst, entziehn sich der Definition; definierbar ist nur das, was keine Geschichte hat." Friedrich Nietzsche, *Zur Genealogie der Moral,* http://records.viu.ca/~johnstoi/nietzsche/zurgenealogie2.htm (accessed April 6, 2013).

114 *the better part of a million dollars.* The loss of the interpretation program was a small nick in a large wound. Cuts to the BC Parks budget since 2001 have totalled about ten million dollars. The current budget, says the Canadian Parks and Wilderness Society, is "the same as it was in the early 1970s when BC's parks system was one-fifth of its current size." To put this in perspective, the thirteen million hectares overseen by BC Parks is the third largest in North America—only the national park systems of the United States and Canada manage more acres. And yet Canada's national system, which handles about the same number of annual visitors as BC Parks, has a budget ten times larger. Canadian Parks and Wilderness Society, "Parks Report 2012" (2012), http://cpaws.org/uploads/cpaws_parksreport_2012.pdf (accessed December 13, 2013), 8.

116 *smooths wrinkles of the old.* From *The Colonist,* July 30, 1880, page 3, cited in Paula Wuorinen, "A History of Goldstream Provincial Park: A Report Prepared for the Parks Branch by the Historic Parks and Sites Division" (July 1976), 14.

122 *except for road, hydro line, railway right-of-way.* Claudia Copley and Darren Copley, "Teacher's Background Information [to Goldstream Park]," unnumbered final page.

125 *millions of acres, billions of feet of timber.* Aldo Leopold, letter to Clara Leopold, October 7, 1909, Aldo Leopold Papers, 10-8, 7. Cited in Curt Meine, *Aldo Leopold: His Life and Work* (Madison, Wisconsin: University of Wisconsin Press, 2010), 94.

125 *after many days of much riding.* Aldo Leopold, "To the Forest Officers of the Carson," *The Carson Pine Cone,* July 1913 (1913): 4, from the Aldo Leopold Archives of the University of Wisconsin Digital Collections, http://digicoll.library.wisc.edu/cgi-bin/AldoLeopold/AldoLeopold-idx?type=goto&id=AldoLeopold.ALForSerPine&page=270 (accessed January 28, 2013).

125   *no such thing as forestry*. Aldo Leopold states this in a book review with the title "*Notes on German Game Management, Chiefly in Bavaria and Baden*. By Ward Shepard," *Journal of Forestry* 32 (October 1, 1934): 775.

126   *a reduction in the predatory animal population*. *The Pine Cone* (Christmas 1915): 2. From the Aldo Leopold Archives of the University of Wisconsin Digital Collections,   http://digital.library.wisc.edu/1711.dl/AldoLeopold.ALPC-Chri1915 (accessed January 28, 2013).

126   *a continuous stretch of country preserved in its natural state*. Aldo Leopold, "The Wilderness and Its Place in Forest Recreation Policy," *Journal of Forestry* 19 (November 1921): 719.

127   *even longer and more complex train*. The word "nature" is "one of the richest, most complicated and contradictory words in the entire English language." William Cronon, *Nature's Metropolis: Chicago and the Great West* (New York: W. W. Norton & Company, 1992), xvii.

128   *incorporates much of the vocabulary and apparatus*. Thomas S. Kuhn, *The Structure of Scientific Revolutions*, 2nd edition (Chicago: University of Chicago Press, 1970), 149.

128   *practice their trade in different worlds*. Thomas S. Kuhn, *The Structure of Scientific Revolutions*, 2nd edition (Chicago: University of Chicago Press, 1970), 150.

129   *a political system that governs people by sorting them into social groupings*. Dorothy Roberts, *Fatal Invention: How Science, Politics, and Big Business Re-Create Race in the Twenty-First Century* (New York: The New Press, 2011), 4.

131   *within itself a principle of motion and stationariness*. Aristotle, *The Basic Works of Aristotle*, ed. Richard McKeon, trans. W. D. Ross (New York: Random House, 1971), 236.

132   *those things which nature is said to do, are by divine art performed*. Richard Hooker, *Of the Laws of Ecclesiastical Polity*, ed. A. S. McGrade and Brian Vickers (London: Sidgwick & Jackson, 1975), 115–116.

133   *based on the principle that the world of nature*. R. G. Collingwood, *The Idea of Nature* (Oxford: Clarendon Press, 1945), 3.

133   *writers such as Nicolaus Copernicus, Francis Bacon, and Giordano Bruno*. R. G. Collingwood, *The Idea of Nature* (Oxford: Clarendon Press, 1945), 5, 100.

133   *printing presses, clocks, and other mechanical devices*. R. G. Collingwood, *The Idea of Nature* (Oxford: Clarendon Press, 1945), 8–9.

134   *we find an increasing alienation between God*. The trends within Cartesianism and the Newtonian synthesis are tracked and compared in John Gascoigne, "Ideas of Nature," *The Cambridge History of Science:* Volume 4,

Eighteenth-Century Science (Cambridge: Cambridge University Press, 2003), 285–304. The eighteenth century, Gascoigne observes, "saw the transition from natural philosophy as a branch of philosophy to the beginnings of an array of scientific disciplines that largely undermined the assumption of a unified view of Nature" (286). On the European continent, "the intrusion of the foreign body of Cartesianism into the traditional philosophical corpus of learning increasingly separated natural philosophy from other forms of philosophy" (286). In Britain, Newton's work "largely abandoned the attempt to construct a model of Nature based on philosophically consistent premises" (288).

134 *wanted to avoid God everywhere in his philosophy.* "Je ne puis pardonner à Descartes: il aurait bien voulu, dans toute sa philosophie, pouvoir se passer de Dieu; mais il n'a pu s'empêcher de lui faire donner une chiquenaude pour mettre le monde en mouvement; après cela, il n'a plus que faire de Dieu." Blaise Pascal, *Pascal's Pensées: Brunschvicg, 1897 edition*, section 77, transcribed by Patrick Q. Moran, http://pascalpense.org/documents/BlaisePascal-PenseeFR.pdf (accessed January 25, 2013).

134 *direct contact with the divine was increasingly relegated to a personal, inner, spiritual world.* In 1784, at the pinnacle of the Enlightenment trend toward the personal dimension of religion, James Madison argued that the religion "of every man must be left to the conviction and conscience of every man; and it is the right of every man to exercise it as these may dictate." James Madison, "Memorial and Remonstrance against Religious Assessments," *The Writings of James Madison*, ed. Gaillard Hunt, vol. 2 (New York: G. P. Putnam's Sons, 1901), 184.

134 *fire had blazed from the personal "God of Abraham, God of Isaac, God of Jacob."* "FEU. Dieu d'Abraham, Dieu d'Isaac, Dieu de Jacob, non des philosophes et savants." Blaise Pascal, *Oeuvres Complètes*, vol. 3, ed. Jean Mesnard (Paris: Desclée de Brouwer, 1991), 51.

137 *the grand untrodden forest.* T. H. Huxley, Letter to Rachel Huxley, April 6, 1850, http://aleph0.clarku.edu/huxley/letters/50.html (accessed February 7, 2013).

137 *representative samples.* Aldo Leopold, "Planning for Wildlife," Unfinished Manuscripts 81–120, page 1229, the Aldo Leopold Archives of the University of Wisconsin Digital Collections, http://digital.library.wisc.edu/1711.dl/AldoLeopold.ALTypeCop (accessed January 29, 2013).

137 *dabbling with some kind of Clements-like organicism.* In an early (1923) essay, Leopold quotes with approval the superorganicism of the mystic P. D. Ouspensky: "[Ouspensky] then states that it is at least not impossible to regard the earth's parts—topsoil, mountains, rivers, atmosphere, etc.— as organs, or parts of organs, of a coordinated whole, each part with a

definite function. And, if we could see this whole, as a whole, through a great period of time, we might perceive not only organs with coordinated functions, but possibly also that process of consumption and replacement which in biology we call the metabolism, or growth. In such a case we would have all the visible attributes of a living thing, which we do not now realize to be such because it is too big, and its life processes too slow." Aldo Leopold, "Conservation in the Southwest," *The River of the Mother of God and Other Essays*, ed. Susan L. Flader and J. Baird Callicott (Madison: University of Wisconsin Press, 1993), 95.

139   *untrammeled by man.* The Wilderness Act of 1964, Pub. L. No. 88-577, 78 *U. S. Statutes at Large* 890 (September 3, 1964), print.

140   *every form of life has value regardless of its worth to human beings.* The Earth Charter, Principle I.1., http://www.earthcharterinaction.org/invent/images/uploads/echarter_english.pdf (accessed January 26, 2013).

140   *adopted and adapted these humanitarian tools to argue for the parallel rights of nature.* For a concise diagram of the way rights have expanded from a human moral sphere to a natural sphere, see Roderick Frazier Nash, *The Rights of Nature: A History of Environmental Ethics* (Madison: The University of Wisconsin Press, 1989), 7.

140   *hanged on one rope a dozen slave girls.* Aldo Leopold, *A Sand County Almanac* (New York: Ballantine Books, 1966), 237-238.

140   *at some point, Leopold suggests, the status of nature will be lifted above low utilitarian goals.* "It has required 19 centuries to define decent man-to-man conduct and the process is only half done; it may take as long to evolve a code of decency for man-to-land conduct." Aldo Leopold, "The Ecological Conscience," *The River of the Mother of God and Other Essays*, ed. Susan L. Flader and J. Baird Callicott (Madison: University of Wisconsin Press, 1993), 345.

141   *instinctively understood as something alien.* Roderick Frazier Nash, *Wilderness and the American Mind*, 4th edition (New Haven, Connecticut: Yale University Press, 2001), 8.

142   *the Wilderness Act of 1964 employed a number of creative synonyms.* The Wilderness Act of 1964, Pub. L. No. 88-577, 78 *U. S. Statutes at Large* 890 (September 3, 1964), print.

141   *in the wilderness, I find something more dear and connate.* R. W. Emerson, *Nature: Addresses and Lectures* (Boston: James Munroe and Company, 1849), 8.

142   *name-calling, conference outbursts.* Michael P. Nelson and J. Baird Callicott, "Introduction," *The Great New Wilderness Debate*, ed. J. Baird Callicott and Michael P. Nelson (Athens: University of Georgia Press, 1998), 4.

142 *we set ourselves up for a major disappointment.* Cronon points out that "It is not the things we label as wilderness that are the problem . . . but rather what we ourselves mean when we use that label." The term *wilderness* serves as an "ideological underpinning for environmental concerns that might otherwise seem quite remote from it." William Cronon, "The Trouble with Wilderness," *The Great New Wilderness Debate*, ed. J. Baird Callicott and Michael P. Nelson (Athens: University of Georgia Press, 1998), 585.

143 *who have been in the area longer than anyone can remember.* Ramachandra Guha, "Deep Ecology Revisited," *The Great New Wilderness Debate*, ed. J. Baird Callicott and Michael P. Nelson (Athens: University of Georgia Press, 1998), 275.

144 *Indian activity throughout the Americas had modified forest extent and composition.* William M. Denevan, "The Pristine Myth," *The Great New Wilderness Debate*, ed. J. Baird Callicott and Michael P. Nelson (Athens, Georgia: University of Georgia Press, 1998), 415-6.

144 *more like a widow than a virgin.* Francis Jennings, *Invasion of America: Indians, Colonialism, and the Cant of Conquest* (Chapel Hill: University of North Carolina Press, 1975), 30.

145 *pesticides and heavy metals accumulate in wilderness food chains.* In the 1990s William Smith of Yale University's School of Forestry and Environmental Studies documented the presence of PCBs, DDT, and DDT breakdown products in the White Mountains' Hubbard Brook Experimental Forest and Mount Moosilauke, in areas far from any known production or application sites. He finds evidence that the chemicals were the result of atmospheric diffusion and deposition. W. H. Smith et al., "Trace Organochlorine Contamination of the Forest Floor of the White Mountain National Forest, New Hampshire," *Environmental Science and Technology* 27 (1993): 2244–2246.

145 *carry more mercury and PCBs in their bodies than anyone else on earth.* Marla Cone, *Silent Snow: The Slow Poisoning of the Arctic* (New York: Grove Press, 2006), 43.

145 *defining wilderness in terms of human absence.* J. Baird Callicott, "The Wilderness Idea Revisited," *The Great New Wilderness Debate*, ed. J. Baird Callicott and Michael P. Nelson (Athens: The University of Georgia Press, 1998), 348. "[The] popular wilderness idea . . . perpetuates the pre-Darwinian Western metaphysical dichotomy between 'man' and nature."

147 *a militant minority of wilderness-minded citizens.* Aldo Leopold, *A Sand County Almanac* (New York: Ballantine Books, 1966), 279.

148   *brainy young technicians.* Aldo Leopold, "Conservation Economics," *The River of the Mother of God and Other Essays,* ed. Susan L. Flader and J. Baird Callicott (Madison: University of Wisconsin Press, 1993), 197.

148   *one of the thousand farm communities.* Quoted in Renae Anderson, "Coon Valley Days," *Wisconsin Academy Review* 48 (2002): 43. The source of the original quotation, says Anderson, is Aldo Leopold, "Coon Valley: An Adventure in Cooperative Conservation," *American Forests* 41 (May 1936): 206–207. At the time when Leopold was part of the Coon Valley project, the agency running the project was known as the Soil Erosion Service. It was renamed the Soil Conservation Service in 1935. See also the discussion of the Coon Valley project in Curt Meine, *Aldo Leopold: His Life and Work* (Madison: University of Wisconsin Press, 2010), 313–314. Meine mentions that two of Leopold's sons, Luna and Starker, were also part of the project.

148   *it is easy to side-step the issue.* Quotation taken from Curt Meine, *Aldo Leopold: His Life and Work* (Madison: University of Wisconsin Press, 2010), 320–321. Leopold's statement, says Meine, is from an undated fragment in the Aldo Leopold Papers at the University of Wisconsin.

149   *an ideal of human unity and harmony with nature.* J. Baird Callicott, "The Wilderness Idea Revisited," *The Great New Wilderness Debate,* ed. J. Baird Callicott and Michael P. Nelson (Athens: University of Georgia Press, 1998), 338.

149   *echoes Thoreau's Walden in style and outlook.* Style parallels between Leopold and Thoreau are easily noted. Philip Connors comments that Leopold's ideas were "expressed with an aphoristic beauty seldom matched in American writing on the natural world." Philip Connors, *Fire Season* (New York: Ecco, 2012), 10.

149   *have destroyed the Indies.* Bartolomé de Las Casas, *History of the Indies,* trans. Andrée Collard (New York: Harper and Row, 1971), 267.

153   *I was searching for something.* C. P. Snow, *The Two Cultures: And A Second Look* (Cambridge, UK: Cambridge University Press, 1964), 9.

153   *gulf of mutual incomprehension.* C. P. Snow, *The Two Cultures: And A Second Look* (Cambridge, UK: Cambridge University Press, 1964), 4.

151   *anchors, with overlapping zones.* Emma Marris, *Rambunctious Garden: Saving Nature in a Post-Wild World* (New York: Bloomsbury, 2011), 136.

158   *one of the anomalies of modern ecology.* Nina Leopold Bradley and W. Huffaker, "Foreword," *Aldo Leopold and the Ecological Conscience,* ed. R. I. Knight and S. Riedel, (Oxford: Oxford University Press, 2002), 8.

Index